MEDITERRANEAN DIET COOKBOOK WITH PICTURES

Easy & Delicious Mediterranean Recipes for Beginners and Advanced Users

Marcie Janes

Table of Contents

The Mediterranean diet is both delicious and nutritious, thanks to its abundance of savoury components such as fruits, vegetables, whole grains, and heart-healthy fats.

It's also linked to a slew of health benefits, including supporting brain function, promoting heart health, and regulating blood sugar levels, among others.

Although there are no hard and fast rules for following the Mediterranean diet, there are a number of general suggestions you can follow to incorporate the diet's principles into your everyday routine.

This article delves deeper into the Mediterranean diet, including what it is, how to follow it, and how it can benefit your health.

What Is Mediterranean Diet?

The Mediterranean diet is based on the traditional cuisine that people in Mediterranean nations like France, Spain, Greece, and Italy used to eat.

Although there are no particular dietary guidelines, fruits, vegetables, whole grains, legumes, nuts, seeds, and heart-healthy fats are often encouraged. Refined cereals, processed meals, and added sugar should all be avoided.

A growing body of evidence suggests that the Mediterranean diet can help people lose weight and prevent heart attacks, strokes, type 2 diabetes, and premature death.

As a result, the Mediterranean diet is frequently suggested to people who want to enhance their health and protect themselves from chronic disease.

Dietary guidelines indicate that persons consume the following foods:

- a wide range of fruits, veggies, and whole grains
- nuts, seeds, and olive oil are all good sources of healthy fats.
- modest dairy and seafood intake

- a small amount of white meat and a small amount of red meat, as well as a few eggs
- red wine, but only in moderation

Antioxidant-rich fruits, vegetables, whole grains, beans, legumes, nuts, seeds, olive oil, herbs, and spices are all part of a traditional Mediterranean diet. It also encourages regular diet of omega-3-rich fish and seafood, as well as poultry, eggs, cheese, and yoghurt on a weekly basis. Red meat, sweets, and other processed foods are not allowed in the diet. In moderation, red wine is recommended, although it is not required. Coffee and tea are permitted, but make sure to drink enough water.

How Does It Work?

As more studies into the health benefits of this type of diet have been conducted, specific items may be discovered to be more important in the future. For the time being, however, it appears that the overall diet approach and variety of foods, rather than individual "superfoods", are what make this such a healthy way of eating.

This makes sense, because if you're eating an unhealthy diet full of processed foods, adding one factor like olive oil as the sole change you make is unlikely to have a significant impact on your health. However, if you change your entire diet to include a bit less meat and a little more fish, choose healthy fats, and eat more fruits and vegetables, you might be able to lose weight.

The Advantages of The Mediterranean Diet

It promotes heart health.

The Mediterranean diet's capacity to boost heart health has been thoroughly researched. In fact, studies have linked the Mediterranean diet to a reduced risk of heart disease and stroke.

One study compared the Mediterranean diet to a low-fat diet and found that the Mediterranean diet was more successful at slowing plaque build-up in the arteries, which is a key risk factor for heart disease.

According to other studies, the Mediterranean diet can help lower diastolic and systolic blood pressure, which is good for heart health.

It helps to maintain a healthy blood sugar level.

Fruits, vegetables, nuts, seeds, whole grains, and heart-healthy fats are all encouraged in the Mediterranean diet.

As a result, adhering to this eating pattern may aid in the stabilisation of blood sugar levels and the prevention of type 2 diabetes.

Multiple studies have discovered that following a Mediterranean diet can lower fasting blood sugar levels and enhance haemoglobin A1C levels, a test used to assess long-term blood sugar control.

Insulin resistance, a disorder in which the body's capacity to use insulin to efficiently manage blood sugar levels is impaired, has also been linked to the Mediterranean diet.

It helps to keep the brain healthy.

Several studies suggest that the Mediterranean diet is good for your brain and may even prevent you from cognitive loss as you age.

For example, adherence to the Mediterranean diet is linked to improved memory and lower levels of numerous risk factors for Alzheimer's disease in a research including 512 persons.

The Mediterranean diet has also been linked to a lower risk of dementia, cognitive impairment, and Alzheimer's disease in other studies.

Furthermore, one major review found that eating a Mediterranean diet improved cognitive function, memory, attention, and processing speed in healthy older persons.

It can assist in the prevention and management of type 2 diabetes.

It may seem contradictory that a diet high in carbohydrate-rich foods like pasta and ancient grains would aid in the management or prevention of type 2 diabetes. However, there are a couple important aspects that make this reasonable: whole grains and carbs from vegetables, which do not alter blood sugar as much as processed carbs, are emphasised in the Mediterranean diet.

The diet also includes a lot of protein and healthy fats.

Too many sweets and desserts are forbidden on the diet.

Exercise is encouraged as part of the Mediterranean lifestyle, which aids with diabetes treatment. The effect of the Mediterranean diet on diabetes risk was explored in a 2014 analysis of nine separate studies, and the researchers discovered that following a Mediterranean diet can reduce the risk of diabetes by up to 19%.

A study published in 2020 backed up previous findings, stating that higher adherence to the Mediterranean diet is linked to a lower risk of type 2 diabetes.

It can protect you from cancers in some degree.

The Mediterranean diet is well-known for its ability to protect against chronic diseases such as diabetes, heart disease, and metabolic syndrome. As it turns out, this anti-inflammatory and antioxidant-rich diet may also protect against cancer.

Breast cancer, stomach cancer, liver cancer, prostate cancer, and head and neck cancer can all be prevented by following a Mediterranean diet, according to a 2017 assessment of studies.

The preventive benefit is "primarily driven by larger diets of fruits, vegetables, and whole grains," according to the authors.

Another study published in 2015 compared the effects of a Mediterranean diet vs a low-fat diet on breast cancer prevention in women. What were the outcomes?

A Mediterranean diet, particularly one supplemented with extra virgin olive oil, has been shown to help women fight breast cancer.

It can reduce your blood pressure and LDL cholesterol levels.

Blood pressure and LDL cholesterol (often referred to as "bad" cholesterol) are two key indicators of health and illness risk. When either marker is abnormally high, it can signal or be a health problem in and of itself.

Fortunately, there are numerous methods for controlling and lowering blood pressure and LDL cholesterol, one of which is the Mediterranean diet. In 2014, scientists looked at the diets of nearly 800 firemen to see how their eating habits influenced key health markers, and they discovered that the more closely the guys followed a Mediterranean diet, the better their cholesterol levels were. A 2018 study found that the Mediterranean diet can lower blood pressure in those with and without hypertension in general, while the authors of the study cautioned that additional research is needed to fully understand the Mediterranean diet's effects on blood pressure.

It encourages weight management that is beneficial.

Mediterranean diets are high in fibre, which aids with weight management. Fibre-rich foods make you feel fuller for longer, which aids weight loss and metabolism. For optimal outcomes, replace carbohydrate items with fibre fruits, veggies, and nuts. The Mediterranean diet's emphasis on real, whole foods—especially those high in fiber—makes it an excellent choice for anyone trying to improve their metabolic health. "A high-fiber diet helps with diabetes and glucose intolerance, keeps you full, and stops you from gaining weight," Gandhi explains.

In fact, the Mediterranean diet has been associated to a lower risk of chronic diseases like type 2 diabetes and metabolic syndrome, and it has been demonstrated to be more successful for weight loss than a low-fat diet.

It enhances gut health.

This diet is abundant in fibre, vitamins, minerals, and antioxidants due to the high intake of whole grains, fruits, and vegetables—all of which can aid gut health by feeding the beneficial probiotic bacteria that dwell there and reducing inflammation. Primates fed a plant-heavy Mediterranean diet had a considerably bigger population of healthy gut bacteria than those fed a conventional meat-heavy Western diet, according to one study. Gut health is linked to mental health, which could explain why a Mediterranean diet is linked to a better mood.

It helps improve the quality of sleep.

Researchers looked into how the Mediterranean diet affects sleep in a 2018 study Trusted Source. According to their findings, following a Mediterranean diet can help older persons sleep better. In younger persons, the diet did not appear to have an impact on sleep quality.

What Foods Are Allowed?

It's debatable which foods fit in the Mediterranean diet, partially because there are differences between countries.

Most studies looked at a diet that was high in nutritious plant foods and low in animal products and meat. However, eating fish and seafood at least twice a week is recommended.

Regular physical activity, sharing meals with others, and reducing stress are all part of the Mediterranean lifestyle.

Fresh, frozen, dry, and canned fruits and vegetables can all be used, but check package labels for added sugar and sodium.

Your diet should ideally consist of the following healthy Mediterranean foods:

Vegetables: tomatoes, broccoli, kale, spinach, onions, cauliflower, carrots, Brussels sprouts, cucumbers, potatoes, sweet potatoes, turnips

Fruits: apples, bananas, oranges, pears, strawberries, grapes, dates, figs, melons, peaches

Nuts, seeds, and nut butters: almonds, walnuts, macadamia nuts, hazelnuts, cashews, sunflower seeds, pumpkin seeds, almond butter, peanut butter

Legumes: beans, peas, lentils, pulses, peanuts, chickpeas

Whole grains: oats, brown rice, rye, barley, corn, buckwheat, whole wheat bread and pasta

Fish and seafood: salmon, sardines, trout, tuna, mackerel, shrimp, oysters, clams, crab, mussels

Poultry: chicken, duck, turkey

Eggs: chicken, quail, and duck eggs

Dairy: cheese, yogurt, milk

Herbs and spices: garlic, basil, mint, rosemary, sage, nutmeg, cinnamon, pepper

Healthy fats: extra virgin olive oil, olives, avocados, and avocado oil

Which Food Should Be Avoided?

You should limit these processed foods and ingredients when following the Mediterranean diet:

Added sugar: added sugar is found in many foods but especially high in soda, candies, ice cream, table sugar, syrup, and baked goods

Refined grains: white bread, tortillas, chips, crackers

Trans fats: found in margarine, fried foods, and other processed foods

Refined oils: soybean oil, canola oil, cottonseed oil, grapeseed oil

Processed meat: processed sausages, hot dogs, deli meats, beef jerky

Highly processed foods: fast food, convenience meals, microwave popcorn, granola bars

Avocado Toast

Prep Time: 10 Minutes
Cook Time: 0 Minutes
Serves: 2
Ingredients:
- 1 tablespoon goat's cheese, crumbled
- 1 avocado, peeled, pitted, and mashed
- A pinch of salt and black pepper
- 2 whole-wheat bread slices, toasted
- ½ teaspoon lime juice
- 1 persimmon, thinly sliced
- 1 fennel bulb, thinly sliced
- 2 teaspoons honey
- 2 tablespoons pomegranate seeds

Preparation:
1. Combine the avocado flesh with salt, pepper, lime juice, and the cheese and whisk in a bowl.
2. Spread this mixture onto toasted bread slices, top each slice with the remaining ingredients and serve for breakfast.

Serving Suggestion: Serve with scrambled eggs.
Variation Tip: Choose perfectly ripe avocados; unripe avocados become hard to mash and aren't flavorful.
Nutritional Information per Serving:
Calories 348 | Fat 20.8g | Sodium 249mg | Carbs 38.7g | Fiber 12.3g | Sugar 37.4g | Protein 7.1g

Strawberry Smoothie Bowl

Prep Time: 10 minutes
Serves: 2
Ingredients:

- 1 banana, peeled and cut into chunks
- 2 cups frozen strawberries
- ⅓ cup whey protein powder
- 2 cups unsweetened almond milk
- 2 tablespoons organic acai powder

Preparation:
1. Place all the ingredients in a high-speed blender and pulse until well combined.
2. Transfer the mixture into two serving bowls.
Serving Suggestion: Top it with granola, chia seeds, and banana slices before serving.
Variation Tip: Cinnamon can be replaced with cardamom.
Nutritional Information per Serving:
Calories: 693 | Fat: 59.2g | Sat Fat: 52g | Carbohydrates: 41.4g | Fiber: 9.8g | Sugar: 24.3g | Protein: 9.8g

Almond Chia Porridge

Prep Time: 10 Minutes
Cook Time: 30 Minutes
Serves: 4
Ingredients:
- 3 cups organic almond milk
- ⅓ cup chia seeds, dried
- 1 teaspoon vanilla extract
- 1 tablespoon honey
- ¼ teaspoon ground cardamom

Preparation:
1. Pour the almond milk into a saucepan and bring it to a boil.
2. Remove from the heat and chill the almond milk to room temperature for 15 minutes.
3. Add the vanilla extract, honey, and ground cardamom. Stir well.
4. Add chia seeds and stir again.
5. Close the lid and let the chia seeds soak in the liquid for 20–25 minutes.
6. Transfer the cooked porridge into serving ramekins.
Serving Suggestion: Serve with fresh raspberries.
Variation Tip: Stir the chia seeds well to avoid lumps from forming.
Nutritional Information per Serving:
Calories 444 | Fat 43.6g | Sodium 28mg | Carbs 15.4g | Fiber 4.7g | Sugar 10.5g | Protein 4.5g

Avocado Milkshake

Prep Time: 5 Minutes
Cook Time: 0 Minutes
Serves: 3

Ingredients:
- 1 avocado, peeled and pitted
- 2 tablespoons liquid honey
- ½ teaspoon vanilla extract
- ½ cup heavy cream
- 1 cup milk
- ⅓ cup ice cubes

Preparation:
1. Chop the avocado and put it in a food processor.
2. Add the liquid honey, vanilla extract, heavy cream, milk, and ice cubes.
3. Blend the mixture until smooth.
4. Pour the milkshake into tall serving glasses.

Serving Suggestion: Serve with pancakes or waffles.
Variation Tip: Use almond or coconut milk for a vegan milkshake.
Nutritional Information per Serving:
Calories 291 | Fat 22.1g | Sodium 51mg | Carbs 22g | Fiber 4.5g | Sugar 15.6g | Protein 4.4g

Yogurt Bowl with Caramelized Figs

Prep Time: 10 minutes
Cook Time: 7 minutes
Serves: 4

Ingredients:
- 8 ounces fresh figs, halved
- 3 tablespoons honey, divided
- 2 cups plain Greek yogurt
- Pinch of ground cinnamon
- ¼ cup pistachios, chopped

Preparation:
1. In a preheated skillet over medium heat, add 1 tablespoon of the honey and cook for about 2 minutes.

2. In the skillet, place the figs, cut sides down, and cook for about 5 minutes or until caramelized.
3. Remove from the heat and set aside for about 2–3 minutes.
4. Divide the yogurt into serving bowls and top each with the caramelized fig halves.
5. Sprinkle with the pistachios and cinnamon.
6. Drizzle each bowl with the remaining honey and serve.

Serving Suggestion: Serve with blueberries on top.
Variation Tip: You can add some orange zest.
Nutritional Information per Serving:
Calories: 276 | Fat: 2.3g | Sat Fat: 0.3g | Carbohydrates: 53.6g | Fiber: 6g | Sugar: 43.7g | Protein: 14.7g

Tomato Omelet

Prep Time: 10 minutes
Cook Time: 5 minutes
Serves: 2

Ingredients:
- ¼ cup water
- 4 large eggs
- Salt and black pepper, to taste
- ¼ cup goat's cheese, crumbled
- 1 scallion, chopped
- 1 tablespoon olive oil
- ¼ cup tomato, chopped

Preparation:
1. Put the eggs, water, salt, and black pepper in a small bowl, and beat well.
2. Heat the olive oil over medium-high heat in a non-stick skillet until melted.
3. Whisk in the egg mixture and cook for about 2 minutes.
4. Carefully flip the omelet and cook for another 2 minutes or until completely set.
5. Place the cheese, scallions, and tomato over one side of the omelet.
6. Carefully fold the omelet in half and remove it from the heat.
7. Cut into two equal-sized portions and serve.

Serving Suggestion: Serve with toasted whole-wheat bread slices.
Variation Tip: Goat's cheese can be replaced with feta cheese.
Nutritional Information per Serving:
Calories: 216 | Fat: 17g | Sat Fat: 7.6g | Carbohydrates: 2.3g | Fiber: 0.5g | Sugar: 1.6g | Protein: 14.1g

Raspberry Oats

Prep Time: 10 minutes
Cook Time: 5 minutes
Serves: 1
Ingredients:
- ½ cup fresh raspberries
- ¼ teaspoon vanilla
- ¾ cup unsweetened almond milk
- 1 teaspoon honey
- 2 teaspoon chia seeds
- ⅓ cup rolled oats
- Pinch of salt

Directions:
1. Add raspberries into the bowl and mash using the fork.
2. Transfer mash raspberries and remaining ingredients into the glass jar and stir everything well.
3. Cover jar with lid and place in refrigerator for overnight.
Serving Suggestion: Add little drizzle of milk and serve.
Variation Tip: Add one to two drops of almond extracts.
Nutritional Information per Serving:
Calories 289 | Fat 11.1g | Sodium 296mg | Carbs 41.8g | Fiber 14.2g | Sugar 8.9g | Protein 8.5g

Eggs with Avocado

Prep Time: 20 minutes
Cook Time: 25 minutes
Serves: 6
Ingredients:
- Olive oil cooking spray
- 1 large avocado, peeled, halved, and pitted
- 3 tablespoons feta cheese, crumbled
- Salt and black pepper, to taste
- 4 eggs, at room temperature

Preparation:
1. Preheat the oven to 400°F.
2. Place two gratin dishes onto a baking pan. Transfer to the oven to heat up for about 10 minutes.
3. Cut each avocado half into 6 slices.
4. Take the dishes out of the oven and grease with the cooking spray.
5. Arrange the avocado slices in each dish and carefully crack two eggs in each dish.
6. Sprinkle with the feta cheese, salt, and black pepper.
7. Bake for 15 minutes until the eggs are cooked to the desired doneness.
8. Take out from the oven and serve hot.
Serving Suggestion: Serve alongside hot coffee or tea.
Variation Tip: You can replace the feta with cottage cheese.
Nutritional Information per Serving:
Calories: 123 | Fat: 10.5g | Sat Fat: 3g | Carbohydrates: 3.3g | Fiber: 2.3g | Sugar: 0.6g | Protein: 5g

Breakfast Quinoa

Prep Time: 10 minutes
Cook Time: 16 minutes
Serves: 4
Ingredients:
- 1 cup quinoa, rinsed
- ½ teaspoon nutmeg
- 1 teaspoon cinnamon
- ⅓ cup flax seeds
- ½ cup slivered almonds
- ½ cup dried apricots, chopped
- 2 cups water

Directions:
1. Add quinoa and water in a saucepan and bring to boil over medium heat.
2. Turn heat to low and simmer for 8-12 minutes or until liquid is absorbed.
3. Stir in nutmeg, cinnamon, flax seeds, almonds and apricots and cook for 2-3 minutes.
Serving Suggestion: Drizzle with little milk and serve.
Variation Tip: If sweetness is desired, add splash of honey.
Nutritional Information per Serving:
Calories 287 | Fat 11.7g | Sodium 9mg | Carbs 35.2g | Fiber 7.8g | Sugar 2.5g | Protein 10.5g

Egg Breakfast Bowl

Prep Time: 10 minutes
Cook Time: 5 minutes
Serves: 1

Ingredients:
- 2 eggs
- 1 teaspoon olive oil
- ½ bell pepper, chopped
- ½ scallion, chopped
- ¼ cup Feta cheese, crumbled
- ¼ cup olives, pitted
- Pepper
- Salt

Directions:
1. In a bowl, whisk eggs with pepper and salt. Add olives, scallion, bell pepper and cheese and stir well.
2. Heat oil in a pan over medium-high heat.
3. Add egg mixture to the pan and let it cook for 2 minutes, then start scrambling the egg mixture.
4. Stir for 3 minutes more.

Serving Suggestion: Garnish with parsley and serve.
Variation Tip: You can also use goat cheese instead of feta cheese.
Nutritional Information per Serving:
Calories 325 | Fat 25.2g | Sodium 992mg | Carbs 9.4g | Fiber 2.1g | Sugar 5.4g | Protein 17.4g

Vegetable Egg Cups

Prep Time: 10 minutes
Cook Time: 20 minutes
Serves: 12
Ingredients:

- 6 eggs
- 2.7 ounces goat cheese, crumbled
- 1 ½ cups spinach, sliced
- 1 red bell pepper, chopped
- ¼ cup unsweetened almond milk
- Salt

Directions:
1. Preheat the oven to 350° F.
2. In a bowl, whisk eggs with milk.
3. Add remaining ingredients and stir well.
4. Pour egg mixture into the greased muffin pan and bake in preheated oven for 20 minutes.

Serving Suggestion: Allow to cool completely then serve.
Variation Tip: You can also use coconut milk.
Nutritional Information per Serving:
Calories 76 | Fat 5.7g | Sodium 68mg | Carbs 1.5g | Fiber 0.3g | Sugar 1g | Protein 5g

Omelet Casserole

Prep Time: 10 minutes
Cook Time: 35 minutes
Serves: 12
Ingredients:
- 12 eggs
- 1 tablespoon olive oil
- 1 teaspoon lemon pepper
- 1 teaspoon dried oregano
- 1 tablespoon dill, chopped
- 5 ounces sun-dried tomato, crumbled
- 12 ounces artichoke, drained & chopped
- 1 teaspoon garlic, minced
- 8 ounces spinach, chopped
- 2 cups almond milk
- 1 teaspoon salt

Directions:
1. Preheat the oven to 375° F.
2. Heat oil in a pan over medium heat.
3. Add garlic and spinach and sauté for 3 minutes.
4. In a bowl, whisk eggs with milk and salt. Add sun-dried tomato, dill, oregano, lemon pepper and sautéed spinach.
5. Pour egg mixture into the greased baking dish and bake for 35 minutes.

Serving Suggestion: Allow to cool completely then slice and serve.
Variation Tip: You can also use coconut milk instead of almond milk.
Nutritional Information per Serving:
Calories 210| Fat 16.9g | Sodium 335mg | Carbs 9.4g | Fiber 3.7g | Sugar 2.1g | Protein 8.6g

Breakfast Chives Frittata

Prep Time: 10 minutes
Cook Time: 35 minutes
Serves: 6
Ingredients:
- 8 whisked eggs
- 1 teaspoon red pepper flakes
- 2 garlic cloves, minced
- ½ cups goat's cheese, crumbled
- 2 tablespoons chives, chopped
- 2 tablespoons dill, chopped
- 4 tomatoes, diced
- 1 tablespoon olive oil
- Salt and pepper, to taste

Preparation:
1. Grease a baking pan and preheat the oven to 325 °F.
2. Mix all the ingredients thoroughly in a large bowl and pour into the prepared pan.
3. Place in the oven and bake until the middle is cooked through, around 30–35 minutes.
4. Remove from the oven and serve.
Serving Suggestion: Garnish with fresh chopped cilantro.
Variation Tip: For a milder taste, omit the red pepper flakes
Nutritional Information per Serving:
Calories 149 | Fat 10.28g | Sodium 210mg | Carbs 9.93g | Fiber 2.3g | Sugar 2g | Protein 13.26g

Spinach and Egg Scramble

Prep Time: 10 minutes
Cook Time: 15 minutes
Serves: 1
Ingredients:
- 1 tablespoon olive oil
- 1½ cups baby spinach
- 2 eggs, beaten

- Kosher salt and black pepper, to taste
- 1 slice whole-grain bread, toasted
- ½ cup raspberries, chopped
Preparation:
1. Heat the oil in a non-stick skillet on medium-high heat.
2. Add the spinach and cook for 5–7 minutes.
3. Add the eggs to the same skillet and cook for 5 minutes, stirring every 2 minutes.
4. Add salt and pepper to your taste.
5. Serve and enjoy!
Serving Suggestion: Serve with the toast and raspberries as a garnish.
Variation Tip: Replace raspberries with your favorite berries or with avocado.
Nutritional Information per Serving:
Calories 296 | Fat 16g | Sodium 394mg | Carbs 21g | Fiber 7g | Sugar 5g | Protein 18g

Quinoa Porridge

Prep Time: 10 minutes
Cook Time: 15 minutes
Serves: 4
Ingredients:
- ½ cup quinoa, rinsed
- 1 cup water
- 1 cup gluten-free rolled oats
- ½ cup unsweetened vanilla almond milk, plus more if needed
- ¼ cup pumpkin seeds
- ¼ cup pecans, chopped
- 1 tablespoon honey
Preparation:
1. In a small saucepan, combine the quinoa and water. Bring to a boil over medium heat.
2. Reduce the heat to low and simmer, uncovered until the liquid is absorbed, 10–15 minutes. Set aside to cool.
3. In a medium bowl, stir the cooled quinoa, oats, almond milk, pumpkin seeds, pecans, and honey until well mixed.
4. Transfer to a storage container and store in the refrigerator, sealed, overnight.
5. If needed, stir in more almond milk in the morning to adjust the texture. Serve.
Serving Suggestion: Top with blueberries and chopped nuts.
Variation Tip: Make sure you use cooked quinoa because raw quinoa has a bitter taste.
Nutritional Information per Serving:
Calories 282 | Fat 9g | Sodium 27mg | Carbs 42g | Fiber 5g | Sugar 5g | Protein 10g

Cheesy Potato Frittata

Prep Time: 10 minutes
Cook Time: 10 minutes
Serves: 4
Ingredients:
- 8 large eggs
- ⅓ cup milk
- ⅔ cup baby spinach
- 2 cups russet potatoes, diced
- ¾ cup white onion, chopped
- ½ cup parmesan cheese, grated
- ½ cup fresh basil, chopped
- 2 tablespoons olive oil
- Salt and pepper, to taste

Preparation:
1. Whisk the eggs, milk, salt, and pepper in a large bowl.
2. Add the olive oil, potatoes, and chopped onion to a skillet over medium heat.
3. Allow the onions to become translucent, then add the spinach, which should begin to wilt after about a minute.
4. Add the egg and milk mixture to the skillet and top with parmesan cheese.
5. Let the frittata cook for about 5 minutes until the edges are brown.

Serving Suggestion: Garnish with rosemary sprigs.
Variation Tip: Substitute spinach with kale.
Nutritional Information per Serving:
Calories 281 | Fat 17.9g | Sodium 329mg | Carbs 15.9g | Fiber 2.4g | Sugar 3.5g| Protein 15.5g

Breakfast Hummus Toast

Prep Time: 10 minutes
Cook Time: 5 minutes
Serves: 2
Ingredients:
- 4 slices of rye bread, toasted
- ⅓ cup hummus
- 1 tomato, sliced
- ¼ cup mixed greens
- ½ cup red onion, sliced
- 1 teaspoon each of salt and pepper

Preparation:
1. Prepare the sliced vegetables while the bread is toasting.
2. Once the bread is toasted, layer with the hummus, tomatoes, onions, and mixed greens to create open-faced sandwiches.
3. Season with salt and pepper to taste.

Serving Suggestion: Top with chopped cilantro.
Variation Tip: Substitute rye bread with whole-wheat pita bread.
Nutritional Information per Serving:
Calories 148 | Fat 4.6g | Sodium 261mg | Carbs 30.2g | Fiber 5.6g | Sugar 3.3g | Protein 6.1g

Creamy Millet

Prep Time: 10 minutes
Cook Time: 15 minutes
Serves: 8
Ingredients:
- 2 cups millet
- 1 cup almond milk, unsweetened
- 1 cup water
- 1 cup coconut milk, unsweetened
- 1 teaspoon ground cinnamon
- ½ teaspoon ground ginger
- ¼ teaspoon salt
- 1 tablespoon chia seeds
- 1 tablespoon cashew butter
- 4 ounces shredded coconut

Preparation:
1. Combine the coconut milk, almond milk, and water in a saucepan over medium heat; stir gently.
2. Add the millet, mix well and close the lid.
3. Cook the millet for 5 minutes.
4. Add in the cinnamon, ground ginger, salt, and chia seeds. Stir well and continue to cook on medium heat for 5 minutes more.
5. Add the cashew butter and cook for 5 more minutes.
6. Remove the mixture from the heat and transfer it to serving bowls.
7. Serve and enjoy.

Serving Suggestion: Sprinkle the coconut.
Variation Tip: Substitute cashew butter with any nut butter.
Nutritional Information per Serving:
Calories 384 | Fat 19.8g | Sodium 215mg | Carbs 42.9g | Fiber 6.6g | Sugar 3.6g | Protein 11.7g

Cherry Oats Bowl

Prep Time: 10 minutes
Cook Time: 0 minutes
Serves: 1
Ingredients:
- ½ cup organic rolled oats
- ½ cup unsweetened almond milk
- 1 tablespoon chia seeds
- 1 teaspoon hemp seeds
- 2 teaspoons almonds, sliced
- 1 tablespoon almond butter
- 1 teaspoon vanilla extract
- ½ cup fresh berries
- 1 cup frozen cherries
- 1 cup plain Greek yogurt

Preparation:
1. Soak the oats in the unsweetened almond milk.
2. Prepare a smooth blend of the soaked oats, frozen cherries, yogurt, chia seeds, almond butter, and vanilla extract.
3. Pour the mixture into two bowls.
4. Add equal amounts of hemp seeds, sliced almonds, and fresh cherries to each bowl.

Serving Suggestion: Top with a drizzle of honey.
Variation Tip: Substitute almond milk with a milk of your choice.
Nutritional Information per Serving:
Calories 889 | Fat 35.3g | Sodium 126mg | Carbs 112g | Fiber 21.7g | Sugar 85.4g | Protein 33.6g

Oat and Berry Parfait

Prep Time: 10 minutes
Cook Time: 12 minutes
Serves: 2
Ingredients:
- ½ cup whole-grain rolled oats
- ¾ cup walnut pieces
- 1 teaspoon honey
- 1 cup fresh blueberries
- 1½ cups vanilla low-fat Greek yogurt
- Fresh mint leaves, for garnish

Preparation:
1. Preheat the oven to 300°F.
2. Spread the oats and walnuts in a single layer on a baking sheet.
3. Toast the oats and nuts just until you begin to smell them cooking, 10 to 12 minutes. Take the sheet out from the oven.
4. In a microwave-safe bowl, heat the honey until it's just warm, about 30 seconds. Add the blueberries and stir to coat.
5. Place one tablespoon of the berries in the bottom of two dessert dishes or 8-ounce glasses.
6. Add a portion of yogurt and then a portion of oats and repeat the layers until the containers are full, ending with the berries.
7. Serve.

Serving Suggestion: Garnish with the mint leaves.
Variation Tip: Substitute honey with maple syrup.
Nutritional Information per Serving:
Calories 916 | Fat 35.8g | Sodium 360mg | Carbs 115.7g | Fiber 7.6g | Sugar 90.9g | Protein 39.9g

Veggies and Egg Scramble

Prep Time: 15 minutes
Cook Time: 8 minutes
Serves: 2
Ingredients:
- 1 cup fresh baby spinach
- 1 tablespoon olive oil
- ⅓ cup fresh tomato, chopped
- 2 tablespoons feta cheese, cubed
- 3 eggs, beaten
- Salt and black pepper, to taste

Preparation:
1. Heat the olive oil in a large pan placed over medium heat and sauté the tomatoes and spinach for about 4 minutes.
2. Add the eggs and cook for about 1 minute, stirring continuously.
3. Stir in the feta cheese and cook for another 2 minutes until set.
4. Stir in the salt and black pepper and remove from the heat.
5. Serve immediately.

Serving Suggestion: Serve with toasted whole-wheat bread.
Variation Tip: You can also add some fresh cilantro.
Nutritional Information per Serving:
Calories: 188 | Fat: 15.7g | Sat Fat: 4.5g | Carbohydrates: 2.6g | Fiber: 0.7g | Sugar: 1.7g | Protein: 10.3g

Yogurt with Berries and Nuts

Prep Time: 5 minutes
Cook Time: 0 minutes
Serves: 1
Ingredients:
• 6 ounces non-fat plain Greek yogurt
• ½ cup fresh berries of your choice
• ¼ ounce crushed walnuts
• 1 tablespoon honey
Preparation:
1. In a jar with a lid, add the yogurt.
2. Add the berries, nuts, and honey.
3. Seal with the lid and store in the fridge for 2–3 days.
Serving Suggestion: Garnish with mint.
Variation Tip: Substitute honey with maple syrup.
Nutritional Information per Serving:
Calories 243 | Fat 4.6g | Sodium 136mg | Carbs 42.5g | Fiber 5.3g | Sugar 36g | Protein 10.6g

Eggs Florentine

Prep Time: 10 minutes
Cook Time: 10 minutes
Serves: 3
Ingredients:
• 2 tablespoons olive oil
• 2 cloves garlic
• 3 tablespoons cream cheese
• ½ cup mushroom
• ½ cup fresh spinach
• Salt and black pepper, to taste
• 6 eggs
Preparation:
1. Put the oil in a non-stick skillet and heat. Mix in the mushrooms and garlic until the garlic is fragrant for about 1 minute.
2. Add the spinach to the mushroom paste and cook until the spinach softens for 2–3 minutes.
3. Combine the mushroom-spinach mixture, then add salt and pepper.

4. Add the eggs and cook, mixing, until the eggs are stiff; turn.
5. Pour the cream cheese over the egg mixture and cook until the cheese starts melting, about 5 minutes.
Serving Suggestion: Serve over toasted bread slices.
Variation Tip: Feel free to add in more seasoning.
Nutritional Information per Serving:
Calories 278.9 | Fat 22.9g | Sodium 191mg | Carbs 4.1g | Fiber 22.9g | Sugar 1.1g | Protein 15.7g

Fruity Quinoa Bowl

Prep Time: 15 minutes
Cook Time: 15 minutes
Serves: 2
Ingredients:
• ½ cup skim milk
• ½ teaspoon vanilla extract
• ½ cup uncooked quinoa, rinsed and drained
• ½ cup water
• ½ teaspoon ground cinnamon
• ½ cup cashews, chopped
• ½ cup fresh blackberries
• ½ cup dried cherries
• 1 tablespoon honey
Preparation:
1. In a preheated saucepan over medium heat, add the milk, quinoa, water, cinnamon, and bring to a boil.
2. Lower the heat to medium-low and simmer, covered, for about 15 minutes or until all the liquid is absorbed, stirring occasionally.
3. Remove from the heat and stir in the cashews, cherries, and honey.
4. Divide the quinoa mixture into serving bowls evenly.
5. Serve with a topping of blackberries.
Serving Suggestion: Top with additional honey before serving.
Variation Tip: You can substitute the blackberries with blueberries and strawberries.
Nutritional Information per Serving:
Calories: 477 | Fat: 18.6g | Sat Fat: 3.5g | Carbohydrates: 66.2g | Fiber: 6.8g | Sugar: 24.7g | Protein: 13.8g

White Bean Soup

Prep Time: 10 Minutes
Cook Time: 8 hours
Serves: 6
Ingredients:
- 1 cup celery, chopped
- 1 cup carrot, chopped
- 1 yellow onion, chopped
- 6 cups veggie stock
- 4 garlic cloves, minced
- 2 cups navy beans, dried
- ½ teaspoon basil, dried
- ½ teaspoon sage, dried
- 1 teaspoon thyme, dried
- A pinch of salt and black pepper

Preparation:
1. In your slow cooker, combine the beans with the stock and the rest of the ingredients.
2. Put the lid on and cook on Low for 8 hours.
3. Divide the soup into bowls and serve right away.
Serving Suggestion: Serve with roasted vegetables and crusty bread.
Variation Tip: Add other vegetables of your choice for a healthier result!
Nutritional Information per Serving:
Calories 264 | Fat 17.5g | Sodium 751mg | Carbs 23.7g | Fiber 4.5g | Sugar 6.6g | Protein 11.5g

Cucumber and Tomato Salad

Prep Time: 10 Minutes
Cook Time: 0 Minutes
Serves: 4
Ingredients:
- Salt and black pepper, to taste
- 1 tablespoon fresh lemon juice
- 1 onion, chopped

- 1 cucumber, peeled and diced
- 2 tomatoes, chopped
- 4 cups spinach
Preparation:
1. In a salad bowl, mix the onions, cucumbers, and tomatoes.
2. Season with pepper and salt to taste.
3. Add the lemon juice and mix well.
4. Add the spinach, toss to coat, serve and enjoy.
Serving Suggestion: Top with feta cheese and chickpeas.
Variation Tip: Remove the seeds from the cucumber if you don't want any bitterness.
Nutritional Information per Serving:
Calories 70.3 | Fat 0.3g | Sodium 50mg | Carbs 8.9g | Fiber 2.4g | Sugar 4.3g | Protein 2.2g

Lentil Soup

Prep Time: 10 minutes
Cook Time: 35 minutes
Serves: 4
Ingredients:
- 1 tablespoon olive oil
- 1 onion, chopped
- 2 celery stalks, chopped
- 1 tablespoon garlic, minced
- 6 cups low-sodium vegetable stock
- 2 (28-ounce) cans low-sodium diced tomatoes
- 1 (15-ounce) can low-sodium red lentils, rinsed and drained
- 1 tablespoon fresh basil, chopped
- A pinch of red pepper flakes
- Sea salt and black pepper, to taste
Preparation:
1. In a pot, heat the olive oil over medium-high heat.
2. Sauté the onion, celery, and garlic until softened, about 3 minutes.
3. Stir in the stock, salt, pepper, and tomatoes with their juices, and bring to a boil.
4. Reduce the heat to low and simmer for 20 minutes.
5. Transfer the mixture to a food processor and purée until smooth.
6. Return the soup to the pot, stir in the lentils, basil, and red pepper flakes, and simmer for about 10 minutes.
7. Serve.
Serving Suggestion: Serve with toasted whole-wheat bread.
Variation Tip: Substitute vegetable stock with chicken stock.
Nutritional Information per Serving:
Calories 211 | Fat 4g | Sodium 336mg | Carbs 36g | Fiber 13g | Sugar 11g | Protein 12g

Cauliflower and Farro Salad

Prep Time: 20 minutes
Serves: 4
Ingredients:
For the salad
* ¾ cup pearled farro
* Kosher salt, to taste
* 2 tablespoons olive oil
* ½ medium red onion, thinly sliced
* ¼ cup fresh parsley, chopped
* 1 medium cauliflower head, cut into bite-sized florets
* 1-ounce parmesan cheese, shaved
For the dressing
* 2 tablespoons fresh lemon juice
* 3 tablespoons extra-virgin olive oil
* 1 tablespoon tahini paste
* ½ teaspoon kosher salt
* 1 small garlic clove, minced
Preparation:
1. Heat a pan over medium heat. Toast the farro for about 5 minutes or until nutty and browned, occasionally shaking the pan.
2. Stir in the water to cover the farro by about 1-inch, sprinkle with the salt, and bring to a boil.
3. Cook for about 25 minutes until the farro is tender but still chewy.
4. Strain the farro using a fine mesh strainer.
5. Transfer the farro to a large bowl and set it aside to cool slightly.
6. Heat the olive oil in a skillet over medium-high heat and cook the cauliflower for about 6 minutes, frequently stirring.
7. Stir in the onion and sauté for about 3 minutes.
8. Remove from the heat and set aside.
9. For the dressing: In a bowl, beat all the dressing ingredients until well combined.
10. Add the farro, dressing, and cauliflower mixture to a large serving bowl and toss to coat well.
11. Serve with a garnish of the parsley and parmesan cheese.
Serving Suggestion: Serve with your favorite main dish.
Variation Tip: You can also add some rosemary to this salad.
Nutritional Information per Serving:
Calories: 286 | Fat: 14.3g | Sat Fat: 2.9g | Carbohydrates: 33.1g | Fiber: 6.7g | Sugar: 4.3g | Protein: 10.6g

Greek Chicken Gyro Salad

Prep Time: 10 Minutes
Cook Time: 7 Minutes
Serves: 4
Ingredients:
Chicken
* 3 teaspoons dried oregano
* 2 tablespoons olive oil
* 1 tablespoon red wine vinegar
* 1¼ pound boneless chicken breasts
* 1 teaspoon ground black pepper
* 1 tablespoon lemon juice
* 1 teaspoon kosher salt
Salad
* 1 cup English cucumber, diced
* 6 cups lettuce
* 1 cup feta cheese, diced
* 1 cup tomatoes, diced
* ½ cup red onion, diced
* 1 cup pita chips, crushed
Tzatziki sauce
* 1 tablespoon white wine vinegar
* ¾ teaspoon kosher salt
* 8 ounces Greek yogurt
* 1 clove garlic, minced
* ⅔ cup English cucumber, grated
* 1 tablespoon lemon juice
* ¾ teaspoon ground black pepper
* 2 teaspoons dried dill weed
* A pinch of sugar
Preparation:
1. Heat the oil in a skillet over medium heat and add the chicken, salt, oregano, and black pepper.
2. Cook for five minutes.
3. Reduce the heat to low and add the lemon juice and vinegar and simmer for five minutes.
4. Continue cooking until the chicken is done. When the chicken is ready, remove the pan from the heat and set it aside.
5. Combine the tomatoes, pita chips, chicken, lettuce, cucumber, and onions in a large serving bowl. Mix and set aside. The salad is ready.
6. Whisk the yogurt, cucumber, garlic, lemon juice, vinegar, dill, salt, pepper, and sugar in another bowl. Mix well. The sauce is ready.
Serving Suggestion: Pour the sauce over the salad and serve with the cooked chicken.
Variation Tip: Marinate your chicken beforehand for a tastier result.
Nutritional Information per Serving:
Calories 737 | Fat 29g | Sodium 1253mg | Carbs 54g | Fiber 6g | Sugar 5.7g | Protein 64g

Pecan Salmon Salad

Prep Time: 10 minutes
Cook Time: 0 minutes
Serves: 4
Ingredients:
- 6 cups mixed baby greens (spinach, kale, and Swiss chard)
- 2 large oranges, peeled, and cut into chunks
- 2 red grapefruits, peeled and cut into chunks
- 1 avocado, peeled, pitted, and chopped
- 2 (5-ounce) cans boneless, skinless salmon, drained
- ½ cup pecan halves
- ½ cup pesto vinaigrette

Preparation:
1. Arrange the greens on a large platter and top with the oranges, grapefruits, avocado, salmon, and pecans.
2. Drizzle the salad with the vinaigrette and serve.
Serving Suggestion: Top with chopped cilantro.
Variation Tip: Swap the pecans for sunflower or pumpkin seeds.
Nutritional Information per Serving:
Calories 459 | Fat 34g | Sodium 191mg | Carbs 28g | Fiber 8g | Sugar 13g | Protein 19g

Lebanese Bean Salad

Prep Time: 2 hours 10 minutes
Cook Time: 0 minutes
Serves: 5
Ingredients:
- 1 (15-ounce) can of fava beans, drained and rinsed
- 1 (15-ounce) can of chickpeas, drained and rinsed
- 1 can (15½-ounce) can of white beans, drained and rinsed
- ¼ cup flat-leaf parsley, chopped
- 3 tablespoons olive oil

- 2 cloves garlic, minced
- 1 lemon, juiced
- Kosher salt and black pepper, to taste

Preparation:
1. Thoroughly combine all the ingredients in a bowl.
2. Refrigerate for two hours to marinate.
3. Serve and enjoy!
Serving Suggestion: Top with fresh cilantro.
Variation Tip: Add chili flakes for a hint of heat.
Nutritional Information per Serving:
Calories 312 | Fat 9.3g | Sodium 418mg | Carbs 44.7g | Fiber 10g | Sugar 1.5g | Protein 13.2 g

Greek Avocado Salad

Prep Time: 10 Minutes
Cook Time: 0 Minutes
Serves: 8
Ingredients:
- 2 English cucumbers, sliced
- 1½ pound tomatoes, chopped
- ¼ red onion, sliced
- ½ cup Kalamata olives, sliced
- ¼ cup fresh parsley, chopped
- 3 avocados, peeled, cored, and sliced
- 1 cup feta cheese, crumbled
- ½ cup extra-virgin olive oil
- ½ cup red wine vinegar
- 2 garlic cloves, minced
- 1 tablespoon dried oregano
- 2 teaspoons sugar
- 1 teaspoon kosher salt
- 1 teaspoon ground black pepper

Preparation:
1. Mix the tomatoes, parsley, onions, cucumbers, avocado, and olives in a large serving bowl. Set aside.
2. Whisk the vinegar, sugar, olive oil, salt, oregano, garlic, and pepper in a jar.
3. Close the lid and shake to get an emulsified mixture.
4. You can add salt, black pepper, and sugar to adjust the taste according to your preference. The dressing is now ready!
5. Transfer the dressing to the salad bowl and toss well.
6. Serve.
Serving Suggestion: Garnish with the crumbled feta cheese.
Variation Tip: Avoid using mushy avocados.
Nutritional Information per Serving:
Calories 360 | Fat 32.5g | Sodium 586mg | Carbs 16.2g | Fiber 7.2g | Sugar 5.9g | Protein 5.6g

Spicy Tomato Soup

Prep Time: 15 minutes
Cook Time: 28 minutes
Serves: 8
Ingredients:
- 2 medium yellow onions, sliced thinly
- 3 tablespoons olive oil
- Salt, to taste
- 1 teaspoon ground cumin
- ½ teaspoon red pepper flakes, crushed
- 1 (28-ounce) can low-sodium plum tomatoes with juices
- ½ cup ricotta cheese, crumbled
- 3 teaspoons curry powder
- 1 teaspoon ground cilantro
- 1 (15-ounce) can low-sodium diced tomatoes with juice
- 5½ cups low-sodium vegetable broth

Preparation:
1. Place a large wok over medium-low heat and add the olive oil, onions, and 1 teaspoon of salt.
2. Cook for about 12 minutes, occasionally stirring.
3. Add the curry powder, cilantro, cumin, and red pepper flakes and sauté for about 1 minute.
4. Stir in the broth and all the tomatoes with their juices and simmer for about 15 minutes.
5. Remove from the heat and blend the soup with a hand blender until smooth.
6. Serve immediately topped with ricotta cheese.
Serving Suggestion: Serve alongside mozzarella sticks.
Variation Tip: Ricotta cheese can be replaced with feta cheese.
Nutritional Information per Serving:
Calories: 120 | Fat: 6.7g | Sat Fat: 1.5g | Carbohydrates: 9.8g | Fiber: 1.3g | Sugar: 2.6g | Protein: 5g

Cheesy Beet Soup

Prep Time: 10 minutes
Cook Time: 30 minutes
Serves: 4

Ingredients:
- 1 tablespoon olive oil
- 6 large beets, peeled and chopped
- 1 fennel bulb, coarsely chopped
- 1 sweet onion, chopped
- 1 teaspoon garlic, minced
- 6 cups low-sodium chicken stock
- Sea salt and black pepper, to taste
- ½ cup goat's cheese, crumbled
- 1 tablespoon fresh parsley, chopped

Preparation:
1. In a pot, heat the olive oil over medium-high heat.
2. Sauté the beets, fennel, onion, and garlic until they soften, occasionally stirring, about 10 minutes.
3. Add the chicken stock and bring the soup to a boil.
4. Reduce the heat to low and simmer until the vegetables are very tender, about 20 minutes.
5. Transfer the soup to a food processor or, using an immersion blender, purée until smooth.
6. Return the soup to the saucepan and season with salt and pepper.
7. Serve.
Serving Suggestion: Top with the goat's cheese and parsley.
Variation Tip: Substitute chicken stock with vegetable stock.
Nutritional Information per Serving:
Calories 309 | Fat 13g | Sodium 1984mg | Carbs 32g | Fiber 5g | Sugar 17g | Protein 17g

Mediterranean Watermelon Salad

Prep Time: 10 Minutes
Cook Time: 0 Minutes
Serves: 6

Ingredients:
- 6 cups mixed salad greens, torn
- 3 cups watermelon, seeded and cubed
- ½ cup onion, sliced
- 1 tablespoon extra-virgin olive oil
- ⅓ cup feta cheese, crumbled
- Cracked black pepper, to taste

Preparation:
1. In a large bowl, mix all the ingredients.
2. Toss to combine everything well.
3. Allow chilling before serving.
Serving Suggestion: Serve with your favorite barbequed meat.
Variation Tip: For a creamier result, add avocado slices.
Nutritional Information per Serving:
Calories 91| Fat 4.3g | Sodium 130mg | Carbs 11.4g | Fiber 0.5g | Sugar 5.4g | Protein 3.5g

Chickpea, Bean, and Veggie Salad

Prep Time: 20 minutes
Serves: 6
Ingredients:
- 1 (15-ounce) can low-sodium black beans, rinsed and drained
- 2 cups fresh cherry tomatoes, halved
- ¼ cup fresh cilantro, chopped
- 2 tablespoons fresh lime juice
- 1 (15-ounce) can low-sodium chickpeas, rinsed and drained
- ¼ teaspoon red chili powder
- ¼ cup feta cheese, crumbled
- 2 medium avocados, peeled, pitted, and chopped
- 1 (15-ounce) can low-sodium corn, rinsed and drained
- 1 (2¼-ounce) can diced olives, drained
- 2 tablespoons extra-virgin olive oil
- 1 teaspoon ground cumin
- ¼ teaspoon salt

Preparation:
1. Add the chickpeas, corn, beans, olives, avocados, and tomatoes to a large bowl and combine well.
2. Mix the remaining ingredients, except the feta cheese, in another bowl until well combined.
3. Sprinkle the dressing over the salad and toss to coat well.
4. Serve garnished with feta cheese.
Serving Suggestion: You can also add some chopped onion.
Variation Tip: Cilantro can be replaced by parsley.
Nutritional Information per Serving:
Calories: 573 | Fat: 23.3g | Sat Fat: 4.5g | Carbohydrates: 75.4g | Fiber: 23.3g | Sugar: 13g | Protein: 22.9g

Zucchini and Basil Soup

Prep Time: 15 minutes
Cook Time: 25 minutes
Serves: 6
Ingredients:
- 2½ pounds zucchini, chopped
- 2 tablespoons olive oil
- 1 medium onion, chopped
- 4 garlic cloves, chopped
- ⅓ cup fresh basil leaves, chopped
- ⅓ cup heavy cream

- 4 cups chicken broth
- Salt and black pepper, to taste
- 2 tablespoons extra-virgin olive oil

Preparation:
1. In a large pan placed over medium-low heat, add the olive oil, zucchini, and onion.
2. Cook for about 6 minutes, frequently stirring.
3. Stir in the garlic and sauté for about 1 minute.
4. Add the chicken broth and allow to boil over medium-high heat.
5. Reduce the heat to medium-low and simmer for about 15 minutes.
6. Sprinkle in the basil, salt, and black pepper, and remove from the heat.
7. Blend the soup using an immersion blender until a smooth puree is formed.
8. Ladle out the soup into serving bowls and drizzle with the extra-virgin olive oil.
9. Top with the heavy cream and serve immediately.
Serving Suggestion: Serve with toasted whole-wheat bread slices.
Variation Tip: You can use vegetable broth instead of chicken broth.
Nutritional Information per Serving:
Calories: 170 | Fat: 13.1g | Sat Fat: 3.2g | Carbohydrates: 9.6g | Fiber: 2.5g | Sugar: 4.5g | Protein: 6g

Carrot Soup

Prep Time: 10 minutes
Cook Time: 25 minutes
Serves: 2
Ingredients:
- ½ onion, chopped
- 2 teaspoons fresh ginger, minced
- 1 teaspoon fresh garlic, minced
- 4 cups water
- 3 carrots, chopped
- 1 teaspoon turmeric powder
- ½ cup coconut milk
- 1 tablespoon fresh cilantro, chopped
- 1 tablespoon olive oil

Preparation:
1. Heat the olive oil in a saucepan on medium heat.
2. Sauté the onion, garlic, and ginger until softened (3 minutes). Stir in the water, carrots, and turmeric.
3. Bring the mixture to a boil, reduce the heat, and simmer until the carrots are tender (20 minutes).
4. Transfer the soup to a blender, add the coconut milk, and pulse until the soup becomes smooth.
Serving Suggestion: Serve the soup topped with the cilantro.
Variation Tip: Substitute water with vegetable broth.
Nutritional Information per Serving:
Calories 259 | Fat 21.6g | Sodium 89mg | Carbs 17.4g | Fiber 4.7g | Sugar 7.8g | Protein 2.8g

Portuguese Salad

Prep Time: 10 minutes
Cook Time: 0 minutes
Serves: 4

Ingredients:
- 1 medium head iceberg lettuce, washed, dried, and torn into pieces
- 4 medium tomatoes, sliced
- 1 medium carrot, shredded
- 1 small cucumber, sliced
- 1 small green bell pepper, seeded and sliced thinly
- 1 small onion, cut into rings
- ½ cup pitted olives (black or green)
- Lemon wedges, to serve
- Fresh parsley, chopped, for garnish

For the dressing:
- 2 tablespoons olive oil
- 2 tablespoons balsamic or red wine vinegar
- Salt and pepper, to taste

Preparation:
1. Whisk the dressing ingredients together in a small bowl and set aside.
2. Arrange the lettuce on a serving dish and top with the tomatoes, carrot, cucumber, green bell pepper, onion, and olives.
3. Drizzle with the dressing.

Serving Suggestion: Serve with lemon wedges and garnish with chopped parsley.
Variation Tip: Substitute the iceberg lettuce with crisphead lettuce.
Nutritional Information per Serving:
Calories 141 | Fat 8.6 g | Sodium 260 mg | Carbs 16.1g | Fiber 4.4g | Sugar 8.9g | Protein 3g

Quinoa Mango Salad

Prep Time: 10 minutes
Cook Time: 20 minutes
Serves: 4

Ingredients:
- 1 cup dry quinoa
- 1 cucumber, chopped
- 1 ripe mango, peeled and diced
- 2 pints cherry or grape tomatoes, halved
- ¼ cup fresh basil leaves, finely chopped
- 2 tablespoons balsamic vinegar
- 1½ cups cooked garbanzo beans
- 5 ounces mixed baby greens

Preparation:
1. Put the quinoa in a fine-mesh sieve and rinse under cool water for a few seconds.
2. Boil 2 cups of water in a saucepan.
3. Add the quinoa and reduce the heat to medium.
4. Cover and boil gently for about 15 minutes until all the moisture is absorbed.
5. Combine the cooked quinoa, cucumber, mango, onion, basil, vinegar, and beans in a large dish.
6. Serve on a mixed-greens bed.

Serving Suggestion: Garnish with fresh parsley.
Variation Tip: Substitute mango with two fresh peaches, pitted and chopped.
Nutritional Information per Serving:
Calories 335 | Fat 3.3g | Sodium 39mg | Carbs 65g | Fiber 10.6g | Sugar 12.1g | Protein 15g

Beets and Walnut Salad

Prep Time: 10 minutes
Cook Time: 10 minutes
Serves: 3

Ingredients:
- 2 ounces beets
- 3 ounces arugula
- 2 ounces bibb lettuce
- 9 ounces romaine lettuce
- ¼ cup dry breadcrumbs
- ¼ tablespoon dried thyme
- ¼ tablespoon dried basil
- $1/3$ teaspoon black pepper
- 6 ounces goat's cheese (preferably in log shape)
- $1/8$ cup walnut pieces
- ¼ cup red wine vinaigrette

Preparation:
1. Preheat the oven to 425℉.
2. Trim, wash, and dry all the salad greens. Tear the greens into small pieces and toss well.
3. Combine the herbs, pepper, and crumbs.
4. Slice the cheese into 1-ounce pieces. Roll the pieces of cheese in the seasoned crumbs mixture to coat them.
5. Place the cheese on a sheet pan.
6. Bake for 10 minutes.
7. Meanwhile, toast the walnuts in a dry sauté pan or in the oven with the cheese.
8. Toss the greens with the vinaigrette and arrange them on plates.

Serving Suggestion: Top each plate of greens with two pieces of cheese and sprinkle with walnuts.
Variation Tip: Substitute dried thyme and basil with fresh thyme and basil.
Nutritional Information per Serving:
Calories 460 | Fat 40g | Sodium 787mg | Carbs 21.4g | Fiber 2g | Sugar 9.1g | Protein 17g

Moroccan Chickpea Soup

Prep Time: 10 minutes
Cook Time: 40 minutes
Serves: 6
Ingredients:
- ¼ cup fresh parsley or mint, minced
- ¼ teaspoon ground cumin
- ¼ teaspoon ground ginger
- ¼ teaspoon saffron threads, crumbled
- ½ teaspoon hot paprika
- 1 (14½-ounce) can diced tomatoes
- 1 onion, chopped fine
- 1-pound red potatoes, unpeeled, cut into ½-inch pieces
- 1 teaspoon sugar
- 1 zucchini, cut into ½-inch pieces
- 2 (15-ounce) cans garbanzo beans, rinsed
- 3 tablespoons extra-virgin olive oil
- 3½ cups chicken or vegetable broth
- 4 garlic cloves, minced
- Lemon wedges, for serving
- Salt and pepper, to taste

Preparation:
1. Heat the oil in a Dutch oven on moderate to high heat until it starts to shimmer.
2. Put in the onion, sugar, and ½ teaspoon salt and cook until the onion softens, approximately 5 minutes.
3. Mix in the garlic, paprika, saffron, ginger, and cumin and cook until aromatic, approximately half a minute.
4. Mix in the beans, potatoes, tomatoes and their juice, zucchini, and broth.
5. Bring to simmer and cook, stirring intermittently until the potatoes are tender for 20 to 30 minutes.
6. Using a wooden spoon, mash some potatoes against the side of the pot to thicken the soup.
7. Remove from the heat, mix in the parsley or mint and sprinkle with salt and pepper to taste.

Serving Suggestion: Serve with lemon wedges.
Variation Tip: Substitute chicken with vegetable stock.

Nutritional Information per Serving:
Calories 120 | Fat 26.9g | Sodium 276mg | Carbs 105.5g | Fiber 28g | Sugar 19.8g | Protein 135.1g

Roasted Tomato Basil Soup

Prep Time: 10 minutes
Cook Time: 50 minutes
Serves: 6
Ingredients:
- 3 pounds halved Roma tomatoes
- Olive oil
- 2 carrots, chopped
- Salt and black pepper, to taste
- 2 yellow onions, chopped
- 5 garlic cloves, minced
- 2 ounces basil leaves
- 1 cup crushed tomatoes
- 3 thyme sprigs
- 1 teaspoon dry oregano
- 2 teaspoon thyme leaves
- ½ teaspoon paprika
- 2½ cups water
- ½ teaspoon cumin
- 1 tablespoon lemon juice

Preparation:
1. Mix the salt, olive oil, carrot, black pepper, and tomatoes in a bowl.
2. Transfer the carrot mixture to a baking tray and bake in a preheated oven at 450℉ for 30 minutes.
3. Blend the baked mixture in a blender. You can use a little water if needed during blending.
4. Sauté the onions heated in olive oil over medium flame in a pot for three minutes.
5. Mix in the garlic and cook for one more minute.
6. Transfer the blended tomato mixture to the pot, followed by the crushed tomatoes, water, spices, thyme, salt, basil, and pepper.
7. Let the mixture boil. Reduce the heat and simmer for 20 minutes.
8. Drizzle with lemon juice and serve.

Serving Suggestion: Serve with bread slices.
Variation Tip: Add chili for a spicier taste.

Nutritional Information per Serving:
Calories 104 | Fat 0.8g | Sodium 117mg | Carbs 23.4g | Fiber 5.4g | Sugar 8.5g | Protein 4.3g

Quinoa and Veggie Salad

Prep Time: 20 minutes
Cook Time: 20 minutes
Serves: 8

Ingredients:
- 1½ cups dry quinoa, rinsed and drained
- Salt and black pepper, to taste
- 1 tablespoon balsamic vinegar
- ½ teaspoon dried thyme, crushed
- 1 (15-ounce) can low-sodium garbanzo beans, rinsed and drained
- ⅓ cup roasted red bell pepper, drained and sliced
- ¼ cup fresh basil, slivered thinly
- 3 cups water
- ½ cup extra-virgin olive oil
- 2 small garlic cloves, pressed
- ½ teaspoon dried basil, crushed
- 3 cups fresh arugula
- ⅓ cup fresh Kalamata olives, pitted and sliced
- ⅓ cup feta cheese, crumbled

Preparation:
1. Fill a saucepan with water and add ½ teaspoon of salt and the quinoa. Bring to a boil over high heat.
2. Reduce the heat, cover, and cook for about 20 minutes or until all the liquid is absorbed.
3. Remove from the heat, and with a fork, fluff the quinoa.
4. Set aside to completely cool.
5. For the dressing: In a bowl, mix the olive oil with the garlic, vinegar, dried herbs, salt, and black pepper until well combined.
6. Mix the garbanzo beans, quinoa, arugula, bell pepper, olives, and feta cheese in a large serving bowl.
7. Sprinkle the dressing over the salad and toss to coat well.
8. Serve garnished with the dried basil.

Serving Suggestion: Serve alongside your favorite meal.
Variation Tip: You can use any beans of your choice.
Nutritional Information per Serving:
Calories: 304 | Fat: 16.9g | Sat Fat: 3g | Carbohydrates: 31.3g | Fiber: 2.7g | Sugar: 3.2g | Protein: 8.3g

Spicy Lentil Soup

Prep Time: 20 minutes
Cook Time: 1 hour 15 minutes
Serves: 6

Ingredients:
- 2 carrots, peeled and chopped
- 2 tablespoons olive oil
- 2 celery stalks, chopped
- 3 garlic cloves, minced
- 1 (14½-ounce) can low-sodium diced tomatoes
- ¼ teaspoon dried oregano, crushed
- 1 teaspoon ground cumin
- ½ teaspoon paprika
- 3 cups fresh spinach, chopped
- 2 tablespoons fresh lemon juice
- Salt and black pepper, to taste
- 2 sweet onions, chopped
- 1½ cups brown lentils, picked over and rinsed
- ¼ teaspoon dried basil, crushed
- ¼ teaspoon dried thyme, crushed
- ½ teaspoon ground cilantro
- 6 cups low-sodium vegetable broth

Preparation:
1. In a big soup pan placed over medium heat, add the carrots, celery, and onion.
2. Cook for about 5 minutes and then stir in the garlic.
3. Sauté for about 1 minute and add the brown lentils, stir-frying for about 3 minutes.
4. Add the tomatoes, herbs, spices, and broth and allow the mixture to boil.
5. Reduce the heat to low, partially cover, and simmer for about 1 hour.
6. Stir in the spinach, salt, and black pepper, and cook for about 4 minutes.
7. Squeeze in the lemon juice and serve hot.

Serving Suggestion: You can serve the soup alongside your favorite rice.
Variation Tip: You can also use yellow lentils.
Nutritional Information per Serving:
Calories: 128 | Fat: 5.1g | Sat Fat: 0.7g | Carbohydrates: 14.9g | Fiber: 3g | Sugar: 4.5g | Protein: 5.7g

Grilled Veggie Sandwich

Prep Time: 25 minutes
Cook Time: 5 minutes
Serves: 4

Ingredients:
- ¼ cup mayonnaise
- Olive oil cooking spray
- ½ teaspoon fresh lemon juice
- 2 small zucchinis, thinly sliced lengthwise
- 2 portobello mushrooms, cut into ¼-inch thick slices
- Salt, to taste
- ½ cup feta cheese, crumbled
- 2 cups fresh baby arugula
- 2 garlic cloves, minced
- 1 eggplant, cut into ¼-inch thick slices
- 2 tablespoons olive oil
- ¾ of a ciabatta loaf, split horizontally
- 2 medium tomatoes, cut into slices

Preparation:
1. Set the broiler on high and grease a baking pan with the cooking spray.
2. In a bowl, add the mayonnaise, garlic, and lemon juice and toss well. Set aside.
3. Evenly coat the zucchini, eggplant, and mushrooms with oil and sprinkle with salt.
4. Place the vegetable slices onto the baking pan and broil for about 1½ minutes per side.
5. Shift the vegetable slices onto a plate.
6. Arrange the loaves onto the broiler rack, cut side down, and cook for about 2 minutes.
7. Remove from the broiler and cut each half-loaf into four equal-sized pieces.
8. Layer the mayonnaise mixture evenly onto each bread piece and top with the vegetable slices, followed by the tomatoes, arugula, and feta cheese.
9. Cover with the top pieces and serve.

Serving Suggestion: Serve these sandwiches with your favorite dip.
Variation Tip: You can use any type of mushrooms.
Nutritional Information per Serving:
Calories: 268 | Fat: 16.9g | Sat Fat: 8.3g | Carbohydrates: 25g | Fiber: 6.2g | Sugar: 8.7g | Protein: 7.4g

Bruschetta

Prep Time: 10 minutes
Cook Time: 15 minutes
Serves: 24

Ingredients:
- 6 kalamata olives, pitted and chopped
- 2 tablespoons green onion, minced
- ¼ cup parmesan cheese, grated, divided
- ¼ cup extra-virgin olive oil for brushing, or as needed
- ¼ cup cherry tomatoes, thinly sliced
- 1 teaspoon lemon juice
- 1 tablespoon extra-virgin olive oil
- 1 tablespoon basil pesto
- 1 red bell pepper, halved and seeded
- 1 piece (12 inches) whole-wheat baguette, cut into ½-inch-thick slices
- 1 package (4 ounces) feta cheese with basil and sun-dried tomatoes, crumbled
- 1 clove garlic, minced

Preparation:
1. Set the broiler on medium and place the oven rack 6 inches below the heat source.
2. Brush both sides of the baguette slices with ¼ cup of olive oil.
3. Arrange the bread slices on a baking sheet; toast in the oven for about 1 minute on each side, carefully watching to avoid burning.
4. Remove the toasted slices, transferring them to another baking sheet.
5. With the cut sides down, place the red peppers on a baking sheet; broil for about 8 to 10 minutes or until the skin is charred and blistered.
6. Transfer the roasted peppers to a bowl; cover with plastic wrap.
7. Let the peppers cool, then remove the charred skin. Discard the skin and chop the roasted peppers.
8. Mix the roasted red peppers, cherry tomatoes, feta cheese, green onion, olives, pesto, one tablespoon olive oil, garlic, and lemon juice in a bowl.
9. Top each bread with one tablespoon of the roasted pepper mixture and sprinkle lightly with the parmesan cheese.
10. Broil for 2 minutes or until the topping is lightly browned.

Serving Suggestion: Top with chopped green onions and fresh basil.
Variation Tip: Switch up whole-wheat baguette with whole-wheat sourdough.
Nutritional Information per Serving:
Calories 73 | Fat 4.8g | Sodium 188mg | Carbs 5.3g | Fiber 0.2g | Sugar 0.4g | Protein 2.1g

Avocado Caprese Wrap

Prep Time: 10 Minutes
Cook Time: 0 Minutes
Serves: 2
Ingredients:
- 2 tortillas
- Balsamic vinegar, as needed
- 1 ball mozzarella cheese, grated
- ½ cup arugula
- 1 tomato, sliced
- 2 tablespoons fresh basil leaves, chopped
- Kosher salt, to taste
- 1 avocado, sliced
- Olive oil, as required
- Black pepper, to taste

Preparation:
1. Divide the tomato slices and cheese evenly among the tortilla wraps. Then add the avocado and basil.
2. Drizzle olive oil and vinegar over the top.
3. Season with salt and pepper.
4. Wrap the tortilla and serve.

Serving Suggestion: Garnish with parsley.
Variation Tip: Add chicken or fish for an even tastier snack!
Nutritional Information per Serving:
Calories 791 | Fat 47g | Sodium 280mg | Carbs 71g | Fiber 16g | Sugar 5.5g | Protein 23g

Zucchini Fritters

Prep Time: 10 Minutes
Cook Time: 30 Minutes
Serves: 6
Ingredients:
- 2 zucchinis, peeled and grated
- 1 sweet onion, finely diced
- 2 cloves garlic, minced
- 1 cup fresh parsley, chopped
- ½ teaspoon fine sea salt

- ½ teaspoon black pepper
- ½ teaspoon ground allspice
- 2 tablespoons olive oil
- 4 large eggs

Preparation:
1. Line a plate with paper towels and set it aside.
2. Mix the onion, parsley, garlic, zucchini, pepper, allspice, and sea salt in a large bowl.
3. In a different bowl, beat the eggs before adding them to the zucchini mixture. Make sure it's mixed well.
4. Place a large skillet over medium heat.
5. Heat the olive oil, and then scoop ¼ cup of the mixture at a time into the skillet to create your fritters.
6. Cook for three minutes or until the bottom sets.
7. Flip and cook for an additional three minutes.
8. Transfer the fritters to the lined plate so they can drain.
9. Serve.

Serving Suggestion: Serve with pita bread.
Variation Tip: You can substitute the eggs for a dairy-free option.
Nutritional Information per Serving:
Calories 103 | Fat 8g | Sodium 216mg | Carbs 5g | Fiber 1.5g | Sugar 2.3g | Protein 5g

Carrot Cake Balls

Prep Time: 10 minutes
Cook Time: 10 minutes
Serves: 22
Ingredients:
- ½ cup old-fashioned rolled oats
- 1 cup dates, pitted
- ¼ teaspoon turmeric
- ½ teaspoon ground cinnamon
- 1 teaspoon vanilla
- 2 medium carrots, grated
- ¼ cup chia seeds
- ¼ cup pecans, chopped
- ¼ teaspoon salt

Directions:
1. Add dates, chia seeds, pecans, and oats into the food processor and process until well combined.
2. Add remaining ingredients and process until just combined.
3. Make small balls from oat mixture and place onto the dish then place dish in the refrigerator for 20 minutes.

Serving Suggestion: Serve chilled and enjoy.
Variation Tip: Add ½ teaspoon of ground ginger.
Nutritional Information per Serving:
Calories 54 | Fat 2g | Sodium 32mg | Carbs 9g | Fiber 1.9g | Sugar 5.5g | Protein 1g

Chicken Caprese Sandwich

Prep Time: 10 Minutes
Cook Time: 6 Minutes
Serves: 4
Ingredients:
*   4 tablespoons olive oil
*   1 tablespoon lemonjuice
*   ¼ cup basil leaves
*   1 teaspoon fresh parsley, minced
*   Kosher, salt to taste
*   2 boneless chicken breasts, cut into bite-size pieces
*   Black pepper, to taste
*   8 slices sourdough bread
*   11 Campari tomatoes
*   8 ounces mozzarella cheese, sliced
*   Balsamic vinegar, as required

Preparation:
1. Add the chicken pieces, olive oil, lemon juice, salt, parsley, and pepper to a bowl.
2. Toss well to evenly coat the chicken in the mixture. Set aside.
3. Heat a skillet with some oil on medium heat. Add the chicken and cook for six minutes on both sides.
4. Drizzle the bread slices with olive oil and toast them in the oven.
5. Place the chicken pieces, cheese, and tomato slices over each slice of bread.
6. Sprinkle vinegar, oil, salt, basil, and pepper over the bread slices and serve.
Serving Suggestion: Top with basil leaves.
Variation Tip: You can use crusty ciabatta instead of sourdough bread.
Nutritional Information per Serving:
Calories 612.73 | Fat 32.06g | Sodium 891mg | Carbs 46.5g | Fiber 2.2g | Sugar 2.4g | Protein 34.4 g

Peanut Butter Balls

Prep Time: 10 minutes
Cook Time: 10 minutes
Serves: 16

Ingredients:
*   2 cups rolled oats
*   ¼ cup unsweetened shredded coconut
*   ¼ cup chocolate chips
*   ½ cup honey
*   1 cup peanut butter
Directions:
1. Add oats and remaining ingredients into the mixing bowl and mix until well combined.
2. Make small balls from oats mixture and place onto the dish then place in refrigerator for 15 minutes.
Serving Suggestion: Serve chilled and enjoy.
Variation Tip: You can also use other nut butter.
Nutritional Information per Serving:
Calories 191 | Fat 10.6g | Sodium 78mg | Carbs 20.8g | Fiber 2.4g | Sugar 11.8g | Protein 5.7g

Veggie Tortilla Wraps

Prep Time: 20 minutes
Cook Time: 5 minutes
Serves: 2
Ingredients:
*   ½ small zucchini, thinly sliced
*   ½ teaspoon olive oil
*   ½ medium red bell pepper, seeded and thinly sliced
*   2 whole-grain tortillas
*   ½ cup fresh baby spinach
*   1 teaspoon dried oregano
*   1 red onion, thinly sliced
*   ¼ cup hummus
*   2 tablespoons feta cheese, crumbled
*   1 tablespoon black olives, pitted and sliced

Preparation:
1. Heat the olive oil in a small skillet placed over medium-low heat. Add the bell pepper, zucchini, and onion.
2. Sauté for about 5 minutes.
3. Meanwhile, in another skillet, heat the tortillas one by one until they are warm.
4. Place the hummus evenly onto the middle of each wrap.
5. Place the spinach onto each tortilla, then add the sautéed vegetables, feta cheese, oregano, and olives.
6. Carefully fold the edges of each tortilla over the filling and roll them up.
7. Slice each roll in half crosswise and serve.
Serving Suggestion: Serve with a healthy dip of your choice.
Variation Tip: You can also use corn tortillas.
Nutritional Information per Serving:
Calories: 282 | Fat: 10.4g | Sat Fat: 3.6g | Carbohydrates: 39.2g | Fiber: 8.4g | Sugar: 6.8g | Protein: 10.4g

Chickpea Spinach Patties

Prep Time: 10 minutes
Cook Time: 10 minutes
Serves: 12
Ingredients:
- 1 egg
- 2 cups can chickpeas, rinsed & drained
- 1 teaspoon ground cumin
- 1 tablespoon paprika
- 1 teaspoon garlic, minced
- ½ onion, chopped
- 1 carrot, grated
- 1 cup baby spinach, cooked & drained
- Pepper
- Salt

Directions:
1. Add chickpeas into the mixing bowl and mash using the fork.
2. Add remaining ingredients into the bowl and mix until well combined.
3. Spray pan with cooking spray and heat over medium-high heat.
4. Make patties from chickpea mixture and place onto the hot pan and cook for 4-5 minutes on each side or until golden brown.

Serving Suggestion: Serve with your choice of dip.
Variation Tip: Add ¼ cup of chopped scallions.
Nutritional Information per Serving:
Calories 60 | Fat 1g | Sodium 143mg | Carbs 10.6g | Fiber 2.3g | Sugar 0.5g | Protein 2.7g

Crispy Chickpeas

Prep Time: 10 minutes
Cook Time: 4 minutes
Serves: 6

Ingredients:
- 30 ounces can chickpeas, rinsed
- 2 tablespoons everything bagel seasoning
- 3 tablespoons olive oil

Directions:
1. Preheat the oven to 400° F.
2. In a bowl, toss chickpeas with oil and spread onto the baking sheet and roast in preheated oven for 30 minutes. Stir halfway through.
3. Transfer chickpeas into the bowl and toss with bagel seasoning.

Serving Suggestion: Allow to cool completely then serve.
Variation Tip: Add your choice of seasonings.
Nutritional Information per Serving:
Calories 238 | Fat 1.2g | Sodium 439mg | Carbs 33.9g | Fiber 6.4g | Sugar 0.2g | Protein 7.3g

Cauliflower Fritters

Prep Time: 10 Minutes
Cook Time: 50 Minutes
Serves: 4

Ingredients:
- 30 ounces canned chickpeas, drained and rinsed
- 2½ tablespoons olive oil
- 1 small yellow onion, chopped
- 2 cups cauliflower florets, chopped
- 2 tablespoons garlic, minced
- A pinch of salt and black pepper

Preparation:
1. Spread half of the chickpeas on a baking sheet lined with parchment pepper, add 1 tablespoon of oil, season with salt and pepper, toss, and bake at 400°F for 30 minutes.
2. Transfer the baked chickpeas to a food processor, pulse well, and put the mixture into a bowl.
3. Heat a pan with ½ tablespoon of oil over medium-high heat; add the garlic and the onion and sauté for 3 minutes.
4. Add the cauliflower and cook for 6 minutes more. Transfer the mixture to a blender, add the rest of the uncooked chickpeas, and pulse.
5. Pour the blended mixture over the crispy chickpea mixture. Stir the mixture and then shape it into medium fritters.
6. Heat a pan with the rest of the oil over medium-high heat. Add the fritters, cook them for 3 minutes on each side, and serve.

Serving Suggestion: Garnish with parsley.
Variation Tip: Use fresh cauliflower as the frozen ones tend to have more liquid, making the fritters mushy.
Nutritional Information per Serving:
Calories 333 | Fat 12.6g | Sodium 65mg | Carbs 44.7g | Fiber 12.8g | Sugar 21.5g | Protein 13.6g

Salmon and Celery Salad Wraps

Prep Time: 10 minutes
Cook Time: 0 minutes
Serves: 4
Ingredients:
- 1-pound salmon fillet, cooked and flaked
- 1 carrot, diced
- 1 celery stalk, diced
- 3 tablespoons fresh dill, chopped
- 1 small red onion, diced
- 2 tablespoons capers
- 1½ tablespoons extra-virgin olive oil
- 1 tablespoon aged balsamic vinegar
- Sea salt and black pepper, to taste
- 4 whole-wheat tortillas

Preparation:
1. Mix the salmon, carrots, celery, dill, red onion, capers, oil, vinegar, pepper, and salt in a large bowl.
2. Divide the salmon salad among the flatbreads.
3. Fold up the bottoms of the tortillas, then roll them up and serve.
Serving Suggestion: Garnish with chopped cilantro.
Variation Tip: Substitute tortillas with whole-wheat flatbread.
Nutritional Information per Serving:
Calories 336 | Fat 16g | Sodium 628mg | Carbs 23g | Fiber 2.8g | Sugar 2.5g | Protein 20.3g

Lamb-Filled Pita with Yogurt Sauce

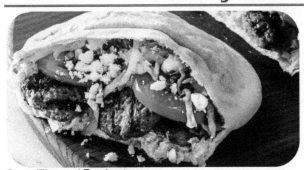

Prep Time: 15 minutes
Cook Time: 6 minutes
Serves: 4
Ingredients:
- 1 tablespoon fresh rosemary, minced
- 2 garlic cloves, minced
- Salt and black pepper, to taste
- 2 teaspoons olive oil
- 1½ cups cucumber, finely chopped
- 4 (6-ounce) whole-wheat pitas, warmed
- ¾ pound boneless leg of lamb, cut into bite-sized pieces

- 1 (6-ounce) container Greek yogurt, fat-free and plain
- 1 tablespoon fresh lemon juice
Preparation:
1. Add the rosemary, garlic, salt, and black pepper to a bowl and mix well.
2. Add the lamb pieces and toss to coat well.
3. Add the olive oil to a non-stick skillet placed over medium-high heat.
4. Transfer the lamb mixture to the skillet and stir fry for about 6 minutes.
5. Meanwhile, mix the cucumber, yogurt, lemon juice, salt, and black pepper in a bowl for the yogurt sauce.
6. Arrange the lamb mixture evenly between all the pitas.
7. Drizzle the yogurt sauce over the top of the lamb and serve immediately.
Serving Suggestion: Top with mint leaves before serving.
Variation Tip: You can also use plain yogurt instead of Greek yogurt.
Nutritional Information per Serving:
Calories: 675 | Fat: 14.1g | Sat Fat: 4g | Carbohydrates: 97.8g | Fiber: 13.2g | Sugar: 3.9g | Protein: 45.3g

Easy Toasted Almonds

Prep Time: 10 minutes
Cook Time: 10 minutes
Serves: 2 cups
Ingredients:
- 1 tablespoon extra-virgin olive oil
- 1 teaspoon salt
- 2 cups skin-on raw whole almonds
Preparation:
1. Heat the oil in a 12-inch non-stick frying pan on moderate to high heat until it barely starts to shimmer.
2. Put in the almonds, salt, and pepper and reduce the heat to moderate to low.
3. Cook, frequently stirring, until the almonds become aromatic and their color becomes somewhat deep, approximately 8 minutes.
4. Move the almonds to a plate lined with paper towels and allow them to cool before serving.
Serving Suggestion: Serve over ice cream.
Variation Tip: Add chili for a spicier result.
Nutritional Information per Serving:
Calories 230 | Fat 22g | Sodium 1163mg | Carbs 6g | Fiber 4g | Sugar 1g | Protein 6g

Parsley Nachos

Prep Time: 10 minutes
Cook Time: 0 minutes
Serves: 3

Ingredients:
- 3 ounces tortilla chips
- ¼ cup Greek yogurt
- 1 tablespoon fresh parsley, chopped
- ¼ teaspoon garlic, minced
- 2 kalamata olives, chopped
- 1 teaspoon paprika
- ¼ teaspoon ground thyme

Preparation:
1. Combine all the ingredients except for the tortilla chips in a bowl.
2. Add the tortilla chips and mix up gently.
3. Serve immediately.

Serving Suggestion: Garnish with fresh chopped parsley.
Variation Tip: Add more paprika if needed.
Nutritional Information per Serving:
Calories 81 | Fat 1.6g | Sodium 39mg | Carbs 14.1g | Fiber 2.2g | Sugar 0.3g | Protein 3.5g

Zucchini Chips

Prep Time: 10 minutes
Cook Time: 12 minutes
Serves: 4

Ingredients:
- 1 zucchini, thinly sliced
- A pinch of sea salt

- Black pepper, to taste
- 1 teaspoon dried thyme
- 1 egg
- 1 teaspoon garlic powder
- 1 cup almond flour

Preparation:
1. Preheat the oven to 450°F.
2. In a bowl, whisk the egg with a pinch of salt.
3. Put the flour in another bowl and mix it with the thyme, black pepper, and garlic powder.
4. Dredge the zucchini slices in the egg mix and then in the flour.
5. Arrange the chips on a lined baking sheet, place the sheet in the oven, and bake for 6 minutes on each side.
6. Serve and enjoy.

Serving Suggestion: Serve with your favorite dip.
Variation Tip: Feel free to add in more seasoning.
Nutritional Information per Serving:
Calories 67 | Fat 8.2g | Sodium 82mg | Carbs 3.9g | Fiber 1.5g | Sugar 1.4g | Protein 3.6g

Butternut Squash Fries

Prep Time: 10 minutes
Cook Time: 20 minutes
Serves: 2

Ingredients:
- 1 butternut squash, seeded
- 1 tablespoon extra-virgin olive oil
- ½ tablespoon grapeseed oil
- Sea salt, to taste

Preparation:
1. Preheat the oven to 425°F.
2. Cut the squash into thin slices and place the slices into a bowl.
3. Coat the slices with the extra-virgin olive oil and grapeseed oil.
4. Add a sprinkle of salt and toss to coat well.
5. Arrange the squash slices onto three baking sheets and bake for 20 minutes, tossing halfway through.

Serving Suggestion: Serve with your preferred sauce.
Variation Tip: Add ½ teaspoon paprika and ½ teaspoon dried thyme for a varied flavor.
Nutritional Information per Serving:
Calories 153 | Fat 10g | Sodium 123mg | Carbs 10g | Fiber 16.4g | Sugar 2.8g | Protein 1.5g

Cauliflower Curry

Prep Time: 10 Minutes
Cook Time: 25 Minutes
Serves: 4

Ingredients:
- 2 tablespoons olive oil
- ½ cauliflower, chopped into florets
- ¼ teaspoon salt
- 1 teaspoon curry paste
- 1 cup unsweetened coconut milk
- ¼ cup fresh cilantro, chopped
- 1 tablespoon lime juice

Preparation:
1. Sauté the cauliflower in heated olive oil over medium heat for 10 minutes.
2. Mix the coconut milk and curry powder, add to the cauliflower, and simmer for ten minutes.
3. Add the lime juice and cilantro and toss well.
4. Serve and enjoy!

Serving Suggestion: Garnish with chives and serve over hot rice.
Variation Tip: Use black pepper for a more vibrant taste.
Nutritional Information per Serving:
Calories 243 | Fat 24g | Sodium 179mg | Carbs 9g | Fiber 2g | Sugar 3.9g | Protein 3g

Spicy Zucchini

Prep Time: 10 Minutes
Cook Time: 5 Minutes
Serves: 4

Ingredients:
- 4 zucchinis, cut into ½-inch pieces
- 1 cup water
- ½ teaspoon Italian seasoning
- ½ teaspoon red pepper flakes
- 1 teaspoon garlic, minced

- 1 tablespoon olive oil
- ½ can crushed tomatoes
- Salt, to taste

Preparation:
1. Add the water and zucchini to an Instant Pot.
2. Seal the pot with the lid and cook on High for 2 minutes.
3. Once done, release the pressure using quick release. Remove the lid.
4. Drain the zucchini well and clean the Instant Pot.
5. Add the oil to the Instant pot and set it to Sauté mode.
6. Add the garlic and sauté for 30 seconds.
7. Add the remaining ingredients and stir well. Cook for 2–3 minutes.
8. Serve and enjoy.

Serving Suggestion: Serve over rice.
Variation Tip: Add in chili for a hotter dish.
Nutritional Information per Serving:
Calories 69 | Fat 4.1g | Sodium 95mg | Carbs 7.9g | Fiber 2.7g | Sugar 3.5g | Protein 2.7g

Balsamic Roasted Green Beans

Prep Time: 10 Minutes
Cook Time: 17 Minutes
Serves: 1 cup

Ingredients:
- 1-pound green beans
- 2 garlic cloves, chopped
- 1 tablespoon balsamic vinegar
- 1 tablespoon olive oil
- ⅛ teaspoon salt
- ⅛ teaspoon pepper

Preparation:
1. Preheat the oven to 425°F.
2. Mix the green beans along with the olive oil, pepper, and salt in a large bowl.
3. Evenly spread the green beans on a baking sheet lined with foil or parchment paper.
4. Place in the oven and bake for 10–12 minutes until the beans turn light brown.
5. Sprinkle the garlic over the green beans and mix well to combine.
6. Bake the beans for another 5 minutes.
7. Remove from the oven and toss with balsamic vinegar.

Serving Suggestion: Garnish with pine nuts.
Variation Tip: Use lemon-flavored balsamic vinegar for a twist.
Nutritional Information per Serving:
Calories 93 | Fat 5g | Sodium 1227mg | Carbs 12g | Fiber 4g | Sugar 3.2g | Protein 4g

Mediterranean Sautéed Kale

Prep Time: 10 Minutes
Cook Time: 10 Minutes
Serves: 6
Ingredients:
- 12 cups kale, chopped
- 2 tablespoons lemon juice
- 1 tablespoon olive oil
- 1 tablespoon garlic, minced
- 1 teaspoon soy sauce
- Salt and black pepper, to taste

Preparation:
1. Add a steamer insert into a saucepan.
2. Fill up the saucepan with water up until the bottom of the steamer insert.
3. Cover and bring the water to a boil over medium-high heat.
4. Add the kale to the steamer insert and steam for 7–8 minutes.
5. Add the lemon juice, olive oil, garlic, salt, soy sauce, and black pepper to a large bowl. Mix well.
6. Add the steamed kale, toss well, and serve.

Serving Suggestion: Serve the kale on its own or add to a grain bowl.
Variation Tip: Add chili for spice.
Nutritional Information per Serving:
Calories 91 | Fat 4g | Sodium 109mg | Carbs 14g | Fiber 2.1g | Sugar 0.1g | Protein 5g

Green Bean Stew

Prep Time: 10 Minutes
Cook Time: 40 Minutes
Serves: 4
Ingredients:
- ¼ cup extra-virgin olive oil
- 3 garlic cloves, chopped
- 1 sweet onion, chopped
- Sea salt and ground black pepper, to taste

- 1-pound fresh green beans, ends snipped and cut into 2-inch pieces
- 1 (8-ounce) can tomato sauce
- ½ cup water

Preparation:
1. In a small skillet over medium heat, add the olive oil and allow it to heat up.
2. Add the garlic and onion and sauté for 3 minutes until the garlic is fragrant.
3. Season with salt and pepper.
4. Add the beans to the skillet and stir gently with a spoon; cover and cook for 10 minutes.
5. Stir in the tomato sauce and water.
6. Cover and cook for 25 minutes more.
7. Serve and enjoy!

Serving Suggestion: Garnish with freshly chopped parsley and serve over rice.
Variation Tip: Use three large peeled tomatoes instead of the canned tomatoes.
Nutritional Information per Serving:
Calories 159 | Fat 13g | Sodium 306mg | Carbs 12g | Fiber 5.4g | Sugar 5.2g | Protein 3g

Cauliflower and Carrot Stir Fry

Prep Time: 10 Minutes
Cook Time: 10 Minutes
Serves: 4
Ingredients:
- 1 large onion, chopped
- 1 tablespoon garlic, minced
- 2 cups carrots, diced
- 4 cups cauliflower florets, washed
- ½ teaspoon ground cumin
- 3 tablespoons olive oil

Preparation:
1. In a large frying pan on medium heat, heat the olive oil.
2. Add the onion, garlic, and carrots and cook for 3 minutes.
3. Cut the cauliflower into 1-inch or bite-size pieces.
4. Add the cauliflower, salt, and cumin to the pan and toss to combine with the carrots and onions. Cover and cook for 3 minutes.
5. Continue to cook uncovered for an additional 3–4 minutes.
6. Serve warm.

Serving Suggestion: Serve with flatbread or rice.
Variation Tip: Make sure to chop the cauliflower into small florets.
Nutritional Information per Serving:
Calories 159 | Fat 0.2g | Sodium 70mg | Carbs 15g | Fiber 4.7g | Sugar 6.7g | Protein 3g

Mushroom and Tomato Bake

Prep Time: 10 Minutes
Cook Time: 20 Minutes
Serves: 6

Ingredients:
- 2 pounds mushrooms, washed and dried with a paper towel
- 1 cup red wine
- ½ cup extra-virgin olive oil
- 3 tomatoes, sliced
- ¼ teaspoon salt
- 1 teaspoon dried oregano

Preparation:
1. Preheat the oven to 400°F.
2. Put the mushrooms in a baking tray.
3. Top with the olive oil, oregano, wine, and salt. Mix well, and then bake for around 20 minutes.
4. Add the seasoning.
5. Serve.

Serving Suggestion: Serve with steak, chicken, or pork.
Variation Tip: Add other dried herbs of your liking.
Nutritional Information per Serving:
Calories 156 | Fat 18g | Sodium 220mg | Carbs 14g | Fiber 2.4g | Sugar 4.5g | Protein 6g

Mediterranean Gnocchi

Prep Time: 5 minutes
Cook Time: 2 minutes
Serves: 2

Ingredients:
- 1 cup chargrilled vegetables, chopped
- 2 cups gnocchi

- 2 tablespoons red pesto
- ¼ cup Pecorino cheese
- ½ cup basil leaves

Preparation:
1. Boil water in a large pot, add some salt and add the gnocchi.
2. Cook the gnocchi for 2 minutes and then carefully drain.
3. Return the gnocchi to the pot and add a splash of water.
4. Stir in the chargrilled vegetables, basil leaves, and red pesto.
5. Top with the Pecorino and serve immediately.

Serving Suggestion: Serve with a side salad.
Variation Tip: Pecorino can be replaced with parmesan cheese.
Nutritional Information per Serving:
Calories: 398 | Fat: 12.2g | Sat Fat: 2g | Carbohydrates: 56.4g | Fiber: 1.1g | Sugar: 0g | Protein: 12.7g

Stewed Okra

Prep Time: 10 Minutes
Cook Time: 25 Minutes
Serves: 4

Ingredients:
- 4 cloves garlic, finely chopped
- 1 pound fresh or frozen okra, cleaned
- 1 (15 ounces) can plain tomato sauce
- 2 cups water
- ¼ cup olive oil
- 1 onion, sliced
- ½ cup fresh cilantro, finely chopped

Preparation:
1. In a big pot on medium heat, add the olive oil, onion, garlic, and salt. Cook until the onion is softened and the garlic is fragrant.
2. Stir in the okra and cook for 3 minutes.
3. Add the tomato sauce, water, cilantro, and black pepper; stir, cover, and let cook for 15 minutes, stirring occasionally.
4. Serve warm.

Serving Suggestion: Serve over rice.
Variation Tip: Replace the canned tomatoes with two fresh and peeled ones.
Nutritional Information per Serving:
Calories 201| Fat 12.9g | Sodium 43mg | Carbs 18g | Fiber 5.8g | Sugar 7.3g | Protein 4g

Roasted Vegetables

Prep Time: 10 minutes
Cook Time: 15 minutes
Serves: 4
Ingredients:
- 1 zucchini, chopped
- ½ teaspoon dried oregano
- ½ teaspoon garlic powder
- 1 teaspoon basil
- ½ teaspoon parsley
- 2 tablespoons olive oil
- 2 small onions, sliced
- 10 grape tomatoes
- 3 bell peppers, sliced
- ½ teaspoon salt

Directions:
1. Preheat the oven to 425° F.
2. In a bowl, add all ingredients and toss until well coated.
3. Transfer vegetables onto the baking sheet and roast in preheated oven for 15 minutes. Stir halfway through.
Serving Suggestion: Allow to cool completely and serve.
Variation Tip: Add your choice of seasonings.
Nutritional Information per Serving:
Calories 168 | Fat 8g | Sodium 314mg | Carbs 24g | Fiber 6.3g | Sugar 15g | Protein 4.7g

Chickpeas with Veggies

Prep Time: 10 minutes
Cook Time: 7 minutes
Serves: 2
Ingredients:
- 2 cups can chickpeas, drained & rinsed
- ¼ cup basil, chopped
- 1 teaspoon Nigella seeds
- 1 tablespoon sesame seeds

- 1 tablespoon olive oil
- 1 teaspoon garlic, minced
- 1 teaspoon chili powder
- 1 bell pepper, sliced
- 1 small onion, chopped
- 1 small zucchini, chopped
- 4 medium tomatoes, chopped

Directions:
1. Add onion and tomatoes in a large pan and simmer over medium-high heat for 3-4 minutes.
2. Add chickpeas and stir well, cover and simmer for 5 minutes.
3. Add bell peppers, zucchini and garlic and stir for 2 minutes.
4. Turn off the heat. Add oil and basil.
5. Sprinkle Nigella seeds, chili powder and sesame seeds.
Serving Suggestion: Stir well and serve hot.
Variation Tip: Add ¼ teaspoon of paprika.
Nutritional Information per Serving:
Calories 487 | Fat 15.5g | Sodium 752mg | Carbs 75.9g | Fiber 16.8g | Sugar 12.1g | Protein 16.9g

Vegetarian Chili

Prep Time: 2 minutes
Cook Time: 30 minutes
Serves: 2
Ingredients:
- 14 ounces oven-roasted vegetables
- 1 can chopped tomatoes
- 1 can kidney beans in chili sauce
- Salt and black pepper, to taste

Preparation:
1. Preheat the oven to 390°F and lightly grease a casserole dish.
2. Arrange the vegetables in the casserole dish and place them in the oven.
3. Bake for about 15 minutes and then stir in the kidney beans, tomatoes, salt, and black pepper.
4. Bake for 15 more minutes.
5. Remove from the oven and serve.
Serving Suggestion: Serve with ready-made mixed grains.
Variation Tip: You can replace the kidney beans with navy beans.
Nutritional Information per Serving:
Calories: 366 | Fat: 15g | Sat Fat: 2.5g | Carbohydrates: 43.8g | Fiber: 15.4g | Sugar: 8.5g | Protein: 14.4g

Tabbouleh

Prep Time: 20 minutes
Serves: 3
Ingredients:
- 3 tablespoons olive oil, divided
- ½ cup bulgur, uncooked
- 2 cups boiling vegetable broth
- 3 cups fresh Italian flat-leaf parsley, chopped
- ¼ cup scallions, chopped
- ½ teaspoon salt
- 3 fresh Roma tomatoes, cored and chopped
- ½ cup fresh mint, chopped
- 2 tablespoons fresh lemon juice

Preparation:
1. In a large bowl, mix the bulgur thoroughly with 1 tablespoon of the olive oil.
2. Pour in the hot vegetable broth and cover the bowl tightly with plastic wrap.
3. Set aside for about 1 hour until the bulgur has softened.
4. Strain the bulgur through a fine-mesh strainer.
5. In a large serving bowl, mix the bulgur and 2 tablespoons of olive oil and the rest of the ingredients until well combined.
6. Serve immediately.
Serving Suggestion: Serve with grilled vegetables.
Variation Tip: Scallions can be replaced with red onions.
Nutritional Information per Serving:
Calories: 244 | Fat: 14.8g | Sat Fat: 2.2g | Carbohydrates: 26.6g | Fiber: 7.7g | Sugar: 5.1g | Protein: 4.7g

Garlicky Mashed Cauliflower

Prep Time: 10 minutes
Cook Time: 3 hours on high
Serves: 6
Ingredients:
- 1 head of cauliflower, cut into florets

- 1 small head of garlic, peeled
- 4 cups vegetable broth
- ⅓ cup sour cream
- 4 tablespoons combined fresh chopped herbs: chives, parsley, spring onions
- Salt and black pepper, to taste

Preparation:
1. Place the cauliflower and garlic in a slow cooker. Pour in the broth until the cauliflower is covered. Add more liquid, if needed.
2. Cover and cook on high for 3 hours.
3. Drain the liquid, reserving it for later.
4. Mash the vegetables with a fork or a potato masher.
5. Add the cream and mash again until smooth.
6. Add some of the reserved cooking liquid to soften the mash.
7. Mix in the chopped herbs, adding salt and fresh ground pepper. Stir to combine thoroughly.
Serving Suggestion: Serve warm with roast chicken.
Variation Tip: Switch up the vegetable broth with chicken broth.
Nutritional Information per Serving:
Calories 83 | Fat 3.8g | Sodium 531mg | Carbs 7.8g | Fiber 1.7g | Sugar 1.7g | Protein 13g

Roasted Carrots

Prep Time: 10 minutes
Cook Time: 20 minutes
Serves: 4
Ingredients:
- 1 ½ pounds carrots, peel and cut into slices
- ½ cup Feta cheese, crumbled
- 2 tablespoons dill, chopped
- 1 garlic clove, minced
- 2 tablespoons olive oil
- 1 teaspoon water
- 2 tablespoons honey
- Pepper
- Salt

Directions:
1. Preheat the oven to 425° F.
2. Arrange carrots onto the baking sheet.
3. Mix together honey, water, oil, garlic, dill, pepper and salt and pour over carrots.
4. Roast in preheated oven for 20-25 minutes. Stir halfway through.
Serving Suggestion: Top with Feta cheese and serve.
Variation Tip: Add 2 tablespoons of chopped basil.
Nutritional Information per Serving:
Calories 216 | Fat 11.1g | Sodium 369mg | Carbs 27.3g | Fiber 4.4g | Sugar 17.8g | Protein 4.4g

Ratatouille

Prep Time: 10 Minutes
Cook Time: 40 Minutes
Serves: 8

Ingredients:
Veggies
- 2 zucchinis, sliced
- 2 eggplants, sliced
- 2 yellow squashes, sliced
- 6 Roma tomatoes, sliced

Sauce
- 1 onion, diced
- 4 cloves garlic, minced
- 2 tablespoon olive oil
- 1 red bell pepper, diced
- 1 yellow bell pepper, diced
- Salt and pepper, to taste
- 28 ounces tomatoes, crushed
- 2 tablespoons fresh basil, chopped

Herb seasoning
- 2 tablespoons fresh basil, chopped
- 1 teaspoon garlic, minced
- 2 tablespoons fresh parsley, chopped
- 2 teaspoons thyme
- Salt and pepper, to taste
- 4 tablespoons olive oil

Preparation:
1. Preheat the oven to 375°F.
2. Heat the olive oil in an oven-safe pan. Sauté the onion, garlic, and bell peppers for about 10 minutes.
3. Season with the salt and pepper, then add the crushed tomatoes. Mix well.
4. Remove the pan from the heat, and then add 2 tablespoons of freshly chopped basil. Stir until smooth.
5. Arrange the sliced veggies on top of the sauce and then season with salt and pepper.
6. Mix the basil, parsley, thyme, garlic, salt, pepper, and olive oil. Spoon this herb seasoning onto the vegetables.
7. Cover the pan with foil, place it in the oven, and bake for 40 minutes.
8. Uncover, and bake for another 20 minutes until the vegetables are softened.
9. Serve!

Serving Suggestion: Serve with seared flank steak.
Variation Tip: You can either cut the veggies into chunks or slices.
Nutritional Information per Serving:
Calories 230 | Fat 11g | Sodium 1112mg | Carbs 32g | Fiber 8g | Sugar 6g | Protein 5g

Vegetable Curry

Prep Time: 20 minutes
Cook Time: 30 minutes
Serves: 6

Ingredients:
- 2 carrots, peeled and chopped
- 6 tablespoons olive oil, divided
- 1 sweet potato, peeled and cubed
- 1 onion, chopped
- 1 red bell pepper, seeded and chopped
- 1 tablespoon curry powder
- 1 teaspoon ground cinnamon
- ¾ tablespoon sea salt
- 1 zucchini, sliced
- ¼ cup almonds, blanched
- 10 ounces fresh spinach
- 1 medium eggplant, cubed
- 1 green bell pepper, seeded and chopped
- 3 garlic cloves, minced
- 1 teaspoon ground turmeric
- ¾ teaspoon ground cayenne pepper
- 1 (15-ounce) can low-sodium garbanzo beans, rinsed and drained
- 1 cup fresh orange juice
- 2 tablespoons golden raisins

Preparation:
1. In a large wok placed over medium heat, heat 3 tablespoons of the olive oil.
2. Add the sweet potato, carrots, eggplant, onion, and bell peppers, and sauté for about 5 minutes.
3. Meanwhile, in another frying pan placed over medium heat, heat the rest of the olive oil.
4. Add the garlic, cinnamon, curry powder, turmeric, salt, and cayenne pepper and sauté for about 3 minutes.
5. Shift the garlic mixture into the pan of the vegetables and toss to combine well.
6. Stir in the zucchini, beans, orange juice, raisins, and almonds.
7. Cover the pan and simmer for about 20 minutes.
8. Remove the lid and stir in the spinach.
9. Cook for about 5 minutes (with the lid removed) and serve hot.

Serving Suggestion: Serve over a bed of rice.
Variation Tip: You can replace the cashews with almonds.
Nutritional Information per Serving:
Calories: 517 | Fat: 21.1g | Sat Fat: 2.7g | Carbohydrates: 70.1g | Fiber: 19.8g | Sugar: 21.2g | Protein: 18.8g

Turkish Beet Greens

Prep Time: 10 minutes
Cook Time: 10 minutes
Serves: 2
Ingredients:
- 2 cups beet greens
- 7 dried Turkish figs, stemmed and quartered
- ½ cup white grape juice
- 2 cups fresh spinach
- 1 clove garlic, minced
- 2 teaspoons olive oil
- Salt, to taste
- ½-ounce parmesan cheese, grated (optional)

Preparation:
1. Cook the beet greens, white grape juice, and figs over medium heat in a pan for about seven minutes before adding the olive oil, spinach, and garlic.
2. Turn the heat down to low and cook for another three minutes before adding some salt.
3. Add the parmesan cheese on top before serving.
Serving Suggestion: Serve alongside grilled meat.
Variation Tip: Add chili flakes for some heat.
Nutritional Information per Serving:
Calories 328 | Fat 7g | Sodium 260mg | Carbs 49.4g | Fiber 10.2g | Sugar 30g | Protein 6.7g

Zucchini and Tomato Casserole

Prep Time: 10 minutes
Cook Time: 40 minutes
Serves: 2
Ingredients:
- 4 cups zucchini, sliced
- ½ cup cherry tomatoes, halved
- 1 teaspoon garlic, minced
- 1 tablespoon olive oil
- ½ cup parmesan cheese, grated
- ¼ cup breadcrumbs
- 4 tablespoons fresh basil
- Salt and pepper, to taste
Preparation:

1. Preheat the oven to 350°F.
2. Add the olive oil to a skillet over medium heat and cook the zucchini, salt, and pepper for 10 minutes.
3. Add the garlic and cook until fragrant.
4. Put the zucchini in a baking dish along with the tomatoes and basil.
5. Top with the breadcrumbs and parmesan cheese.
6. Bake for 30 minutes.
Serving Suggestion: Garnish with fresh basil.
Variation Tip: Feel free to add your favorite herbs.
Nutritional Information per Serving:
Calories 185 | Fat 9.7g | Sodium 302mg | Carbs 20.4g | Fiber 4.2g | Sugar 6.8g | Protein 7.3g

Spelt-Stuffed Peppers

Prep Time: 20 minutes
Cook Time: 25 minutes
Serves: 4
Ingredients:
- 4 large red peppers, halved and deseeded
- ½ cup sundried tomatoes
- 2 tablespoons olive oil
- 1 red onion, spiralized on the flat blade of the spiralizer
- 1 large zucchini, spiralized into thin noodles
- 9-ounce pouch pre-cooked spelt
- ½ cup mixed olives
- ½ cup basil, chopped
- Salt and black pepper, to taste
Preparation:
1. Preheat the oven to 390°F and lightly grease a roasting tray.
2. Arrange the red peppers on the roasting tray, cut-side up, and sprinkle with 1 tablespoon of olive oil.
3. Season with salt and black pepper, and bake for 25 minutes.
4. In the meantime, in a pan placed over medium heat, heat the rest of the olive oil and add the spiralized onion.
5. Cook for 3 minutes until softened and transfer to a bowl.
6. Stir in the zucchini, spelt, olives, sundried tomatoes, and basil.
7. Generously fill the red peppers with the mixture.
8. Roast for approximately 5 minutes and serve.
Serving Suggestion: Serve with a green salad.
Variation Tip: You can use any other variety of tomatoes too.
Nutritional Information per Serving:
Calories: 412 | Fat: 12.5g | Sat Fat: 1.5g | Carbohydrates: 64.3g | Fiber: 12.4g | Sugar: 7.6g | Protein: 12.2g

Roasted Brussels Sprouts and Pecans

Prep Time: 10 minutes
Cook Time: 3 hours
Serves: 4
Ingredients:
- 1½ pounds fresh Brussels sprouts
- 4 tablespoons olive oil
- 4 cloves garlic, minced
- 3 tablespoons water
- Salt and pepper, to taste
- ½ cup pecans, chopped

Preparation:
1. Place all ingredients in an Instant Pot or pressure cooker. Stir to combine well.
2. Close the lid and ensure the steam release valve is set to vent.
3. Slow cook for 3 hours.
4. Serve with a dash of lemon juice.

Serving Suggestion: Serve with grilled meat.
Variation Tip: You can use chestnuts or walnuts instead of pecans.
Nutritional Information per Serving:
Calories 161 | Fat 13.1g | Sodium 43mg | Carbs 10.2g | Fiber 6.8g | Sugar 3.8g | Protein 4.1g

White Beans with Tomato and Arugula

Prep Time: 10 minutes
Cook Time: 5 minutes
Serves: 6
Ingredients:

- 30 ounces can, Cannellini beans, drained & rinsed
- 1 teaspoon dried thyme
- 5 ounces baby arugula
- 1 tablespoon olive oil
- ½ cup sun-dried tomatoes, drained
- Pepper
- Salt

Directions:
1. Heat oil in a pot over medium-high heat.
2. Add arugula and stir until wilted, about 3 minutes.
3. Add thyme, beans, tomatoes, pepper, and salt and cook for 2-3 minutes.

Serving Suggestion: Stir well and serve warm.
Variation Tip: You can also use cooked spinach instead of arugula.
Nutritional Information per Serving:
Calories 133 | Fat 3.5g | Sodium 76mg | Carbs 19.1g | Fiber 5.7g | Sugar 0.9g | Protein 7g

Garlic Cauliflower and Zucchini

Prep Time: 10 minutes
Cook Time: 8 minutes
Serves: 2
Ingredients:
- 1 cup cauliflower florets
- ½ teaspoon cumin
- 1 teaspoon mint
- 2 garlic cloves
- 1 tablespoon olive oil
- 1 bell pepper, sliced
- 1 cup zucchini, chopped
- Pepper
- Salt

Directions:
1. Heat oil in a pan over medium heat.
2. Add vegetables, garlic, cumin, pepper and salt to the pan and stir well.
3. Cover and cook for 3-4 minutes.
4. Remove cover and stir well and cook for 2 minutes more. Remove pan from heat.

Serving Suggestion: Allow to cool completely then serve.
Variation Tip: Drizzle with tablespoon of fresh lemon juice.
Nutritional Information per Serving:
Calories 108 | Fat 7.5g | Sodium 101mg | Carbs 10.4g | Fiber 2.9g | Sugar 5.2g | Protein 2.6g

Cherry Tomatoes and Black Beans

Prep Time: 10 minutes
Cook Time: 15 minutes
Serves: 2
Ingredients:
- 1 (15-ounce) can black beans, undrained
- 1 cup cherry tomatoes, halved
- 1 teaspoon salt
- 1 tablespoon dried oregano
- 1 teaspoon red pepper flakes

Preparation:
1. Pour the black beans and their liquid into a large skillet and bring to a low boil over medium-high heat.
2. Reduce the heat to low and simmer for 5 minutes.
3. Stir in the cherry tomatoes, salt, oregano, and red pepper flakes, and cook for 10 minutes.
4. Serve and enjoy.
Serving Suggestion: Serve over hot rice.
Variation Tip: Feel free to add in other spices.
Nutritional Information per Serving:
Calories 185 | Fat 1g | Sodium 987mg | Carbs 34g | Fiber 12g | Sugar 2g | Protein 12g

Baked Black-Eyed Peas

Prep Time: 15 minutes
Cook Time: 35 minutes
Serves: 3
Ingredients:
- 2 (15-ounce) cans black-eyed peas, drained and rinsed
- 3 tablespoons extra-virgin olive oil
- Salt, to taste
- 2 teaspoons Za'atar
- 2 teaspoons sumac
- 2 teaspoons harissa

Preparation:
1. Preheat the oven to 400°F.

2. Place the black-eyed peas on a baking sheet and drizzle with the olive oil.
3. Season with salt and toss to coat well.
4. Bake for about 35 minutes, shaking the baking pan three times during the cooking time.
5. Remove from the oven and season with the Za'atar, sumac, and harissa.
6. Serve warm.
Serving Suggestion: Serve as a snack with tea.
Variation Tip: You can use seasonings of your choice.
Nutritional Information per Serving:
Calories: 478 | Fat: 18.5g | Sat Fat: 2.3g | Carbohydrates: 66.1g | Fiber: 13.1g | Sugar: 0.9g | Protein: 14.9g

Mediterranean White Beans

Prep Time: 10 minutes
Cook Time: 20 minutes
Serves: 4
Ingredients:
- ¼ cup extra-virgin olive oil
- 1 (24-ounce) jar white beans, drained and rinsed
- ½ cup onion, chopped
- 1 large garlic clove, minced
- 1 teaspoon salt
- ½ teaspoon dried rosemary, crushed
- ½ cup celery, chopped
- 1 (16-ounce) can diced tomatoes, with juice
- 1 teaspoon sugar
- ¼ cup fresh Italian parsley, chopped

Preparation:
1. Heat the olive oil in a skillet placed over medium-high heat and sauté the garlic and onion for about 5 minutes.
2. Add the white beans, tomatoes, rosemary, salt, and sugar, and let the mixture come to a boil.
3. Reduce the heat, cover with a lid, and simmer for about 15 minutes.
4. Stir in the parsley and serve.
Serving Suggestion: Serve as a tasty side dish for pork or chicken.
Variation Tip: Almond milk can be replaced with coconut milk.
Nutritional Information per Serving:
Calories: 346 | Fat: 8.3g | Sat Fat: 1.3g | Carbohydrates: 60.2g | Fiber: 2.1g | Sugar: 1.8g |Protein: 7.9g

Spicy Borlotti Beans

Prep Time: 12 hours 10 minutes
Cook Time: 1 hour 50 minutes
Serves: 8

Ingredients:
- 1-pound dried borlotti beans, soaked overnight, drained, and rinsed
- 1 teaspoon salt, divided
- 2 tablespoons extra-virgin olive oil
- 1 large onion, chopped
- ½ green bell pepper, seeded and chopped
- 1 (14.5-ounce) can diced tomatoes, undrained
- 3 garlic cloves, minced
- 1 (1-inch) piece fresh red chili, seeded and minced
- ¼ teaspoon freshly ground black pepper
- ¼ teaspoon red pepper flakes

Preparation:
1. Put the beans in a large pot, cover with water, and add ½ teaspoon of salt.
2. Bring to a boil over medium-high heat, then reduce the heat to low and simmer for 1–1½ hours, until the beans soften. Drain.
3. In a large skillet, heat the olive oil over medium heat. Cook the onion and bell pepper for about 10 minutes until softened.
4. Add the beans, tomatoes and their juices, garlic, chili, remaining ½ teaspoon of salt, black pepper, and red pepper flakes.
5. Bring to a boil, then reduce the heat and simmer for 10 minutes.

Serving Suggestion: Garnish with chopped cilantro.
Variation Tip: For a milder taste, omit the red chili.
Nutritional Information per Serving:
Calories 240 | Fat 4g | Sodium 335mg | Carbs 39g | Fiber 13g | Sugar 3g | Protein 13g

Black-Eyed Peas Stew

Prep Time: 10 minutes
Cook Time: 55 minutes
Serves: 6

Ingredients:
- 2 tablespoons olive oil
- 4 garlic cloves, chopped
- 30 ounces black-eyed peas
- 1 yellow onion, chopped
- 1 green bell pepper, chopped
- 15 ounces tomato, diced
- 3 carrots, chopped
- 1 tablespoon lime juice
- 2 cups water
- 1½ teaspoons ground cumin
- 1 bay leaf
- 1 teaspoon dried oregano
- Kosher salt, to taste
- ½ teaspoon red pepper flakes
- ½ teaspoon paprika
- Black pepper, to taste
- 1 cup fresh parsley, chopped

Preparation:
1. Sauté the garlic and onions in the oil in a heated Dutch oven over medium flame for 5 minutes, constantly stirring.
2. Stir in the tomatoes, pepper, water, spices, bay leaf, and salt. Let it simmer.
3. Mix in the black-eyed peas and cook for 5 more minutes.
4. Cover and reduce the flame. Simmer for 30 more minutes.
5. Squeeze in the lime juice and mix.
6. Serve and enjoy.

Serving Suggestion: Garnish with parsley.
Variation Tip: Substitute water with vegetable broth.
Nutritional Information per Serving:
Calories 197 | Fat 6.3 g | Sodium 92mg | Carbs 30.4g | Fiber 7.7g | Sugar 5.4g | Protein 8.9g

Gigante Beans in Tomato Sauce

Prep Time: 10 minutes
Cook Time: 5 minutes
Serves: 2

Ingredients:
- 1 (12-ounce) jar gigante beans, undrained
- 6 ounces tomato paste
- ¾ cup water
- ½ teaspoon dried oregano

Preparation:
1. Pour the beans and their liquid into a small saucepan and bring to a boil over medium-high heat.
2. Remove the pan from the heat and drain the liquid.
3. In another small saucepan, combine the tomato paste and water and bring to a simmer to heat through.
4. Arrange the beans on a serving dish.
5. Spoon over the tomato sauce and enjoy.

Serving Suggestion: Sprinkle with the dried oregano.
Variation Tip: If you can't find gigante beans, good substitutes are corona beans or large butter beans.
Nutritional Information per Serving:
Calories 238 | Fat 1g | Sodium 616mg | Carbs 46g | Fiber 12g | Sugar 11g | Protein 15g

Cannellini Beans and Farro Stew

Prep Time: 20 minutes
Cook Time: 45 minutes
Serves: 6

Ingredients:
- 1 cup carrots, peeled and chopped
- 2 tablespoons olive oil
- 1 cup celery, chopped
- 4 garlic cloves, minced
- 1 cup uncooked farro, rinsed
- 1 bay leaf
- Salt, to taste
- 4 cups fresh kale, chopped
- 1 tablespoon lemon juice, fresh
- 1 cup yellow onion, chopped
- 1 (14½-ounce) can diced tomatoes
- ½ cup fresh parsley sprigs
- 1 teaspoon dried oregano
- 5 cups low-sodium vegetable broth
- 1 (15-ounce) can low-sodium cannellini beans, rinsed and drained
- ½ cup feta cheese, crumbled

Preparation:
1. In a large pan placed over medium-high heat, heat the oil and sauté the celery, carrots, garlic, and onion for about 3 minutes.
2. Stir in the farro, tomatoes, parsley sprigs, oregano, bay leaf, broth, and salt, and let it come to a boil.
3. Reduce the heat to medium-low, cover, and simmer for about 20 minutes.
4. Discard the parsley sprigs and stir in the kale, cooking for about 15 minutes.
5. Stir in the cannellini beans and cook for about 5 minutes until thoroughly heated.
6. Discard the bay leaf and squeeze in the lemon juice.
7. Remove from the heat and serve topped with feta cheese.

Serving Suggestion: Serve with yellow rice.
Variation Tip: Kale can be replaced with spinach.
Nutritional Information per Serving:
Calories: 520 | Fat: 10.5g | Sat Fat: 3g | Carbohydrates: 79.1g | Fiber: 22.6g | Sugar: 6.5g | Protein: 30g

Kale Fried Rice

Prep Time: 10 minutes
Cook Time: 15 minutes
Serves: 2

Ingredients:
- 2 eggs, whisked together with some salt
- 2 tablespoons coconut oil
- ¾ cup green onions, chopped
- 2 garlic cloves, minced
- 1 cup vegetables, chopped (Brussels sprouts, carrot, bell pepper), optional
- 1 bunch kale
- ¾ cup unsweetened coconut flakes
- ¼ teaspoon sea salt
- 2 teaspoons low-sodium soy sauce
- 2 cups brown rice, cooked
- 1 lime, halved
- 2 teaspoons sriracha or chili garlic sauce
- Chopped fresh parsley, for garnish

Preparation:
1. Heat a wok over medium to high heat.
2. Add a teaspoon of oil. Coat the bottom of the wok.
3. Pour in the eggs and cook. Stir frequently. The eggs should be scrambled.
4. Transfer the eggs to a bowl. Add a teaspoon of oil to your wok.
5. Add the onions, garlic, and optional vegetables. Cook for 30 seconds.
6. Add the kale and cook for a minute more. Transfer the wok contents to the bowl of eggs. Add the remaining kale to your wok.
7. Now, pour in the coconut flakes. Cook while stirring for 30 seconds.
8. Add the rice. Cook for 3 minutes, stirring occasionally. Pour the bowl contents back into your wok.
9. Use a spoon or spatula to break up the scrambled egg.
10. Add the chili garlic sauce and the juice from the half lime. Combine well.
11. Divide the rice into serving bowls.

Serving Suggestion: Garnish with chopped parsley and lime wedges.
Variation Tip: Switch up the coconut oil with olive oil.
Nutritional Information per Serving:
Calories 934 | Fat 60g | Sodium 260mg | Carbs 154g | Fiber 12g | Sugar 4g | Protein 26g

Cauliflower Rice

Prep Time: 10 minutes
Cook Time: 35 minutes
Serves: 4

Ingredients:
- 1 cup pumpkin, grated
- 2 cups cauliflower, grated
- 4 tablespoons olive oil
- 1 small white onion, chopped
- 1 teaspoon ginger paste
- ¼ teaspoon turmeric powder
- 1 teaspoon curry powder
- 1 teaspoon red chili powder
- $^1/_3$ cup vegetable broth
- ½ cup snow peas
- ½ cup coconut milk

Preparation:
1. In a large non-stick skillet, heat the olive oil.
2. Add the onions and sauté for a few minutes.
3. Add the ginger and cook until fragrant.
4. Next, add the peas along with the vegetable broth. Cover the skillet and simmer for 10 minutes on medium flame.
5. Remove the lid and add the pumpkin and cook for about 10 minutes.
6. Pour in the coconut milk.
7. Add the curry powder, turmeric powder, and chili powder. Next, add the grated cauliflower. Cover the skillet with a lid and cook for 12 minutes.
8. Serve warm.

Serving Suggestion: Top with chopped green onions.

Variation Tip: Omit red chili powder for a milder taste.

Nutritional Information per Serving:
Calories 247 | Fat 21.8g | Sodium 95mg | Carbs 13.5g | Fiber 5.1g | Sugar 5.9g | Protein 3.8g

1. Mix in the cucumbers, tomatoes, vinegar, and remaining oil, then season with sea salt and black pepper.
2. Finally, cover with the cheese, parsley, and mint.

Serving Suggestion: Garnish with thyme sprigs.

Variation Tip: Substitute sherry vinegar with red wine vinegar.

Nutritional Information per Serving:
Calories 359 | Fat 20.9g | Sodium 375mg | Carbs 36.5g | Fiber 3.2g | Sugar 3.7g | Protein 8.9g

Sweet Red Lentils

Prep Time: 10 minutes
Cook Time: 15 minutes
Serves: 4

Ingredients:
For the sauce:
- 2 cups water
- 2 tablespoons brown sugar
- ¼ cup coconut aminos
- 2 garlic cloves, chopped
- ½ teaspoon crushed red pepper
- 1 tablespoon fresh ginger, minced
- 1 teaspoon olive oil

For the lentils:
- 1 tablespoon olive oil
- ½ yellow onion, chopped
- 1 cup red lentils
- 2 green onions, sliced, for serving

Preparation:
1. In a jar, mix all the sauce ingredients.
2. Pour the oil into a large pot over medium-high heat.
3. Add the onion and sauté for about 3 minutes.
4. Once the onion begins to brown and becomes soft, add the sauce and lentils and bring to a gentle boil. Simmer, cover, and cook for about 8–10 minutes.
5. Wait until the lentils are tender and the liquid is absorbed (mostly).
6. Serve hot.

Serving Suggestion: Garnish with parsley and green onions.

Variation Tip: Omit crushed red pepper for a milder taste.

Nutritional Information per Serving:
Calories 277 | Fat 7.7g | Sodium 27mg | Carbs 39.7g | Fiber 15.4g | Sugar 6.2g | Protein 12.9g

Kidney Beans Meal

Prep Time: 10 Minutes
Cook Time: 0 Minutes
Serves: 6
Ingredients:
- 1 can (15 ounces) kidney beans, drained and rinsed
- ½ English cucumber, chopped
- 1 medium heirloom tomato, chopped
- 1 bunch fresh cilantro, stems removed and chopped
- 1 red onion, chopped
- 1 large lime, juiced
- 3 tablespoons extra-virgin olive oil
- 1 teaspoon Dijon mustard
- ½ teaspoon fresh garlic paste
- 1 teaspoon sumac
- Salt and pepper, to taste

Preparation:
1. In a medium-sized bowl, add the kidney beans, chopped veggies, and cilantro.
2. Take a small bowl and make the vinaigrette by adding the lime juice, oil, garlic paste, pepper, mustard, and sumac.
3. Pour the vinaigrette over the salad and give it a gentle stir.
4. Add some salt and pepper. Cover the bowl and allow it to chill for half an hour.
5. Serve and enjoy!

Serving Suggestion: Drizzle with some balsamic vinegar.
Variation Tip: You can use garbanzo, white, or black beans.
Nutritional Information per Serving:
Calories 74 | Fat 0.7g | Sodium 313mg | Carbs 16g | Fiber 5.8g | Sugar 3.6g | Protein 5.5g

Barley Pilaf

Prep Time: 10 minutes
Cook Time: 45 minutes

Serves: 5
Ingredients:
- ¼ cup fresh parsley, minced
- 1 small onion, finely chopped
- 1½ cups pearl barley, rinsed
- 1½ teaspoons lemon juice
- 1½ teaspoons fresh thyme, minced
- 2 garlic cloves, minced
- 2 tablespoons fresh chives, minced
- 2½ cups water
- 3 tablespoons extra-virgin olive oil
- Salt and pepper, to taste

Preparation:
1. Heat the oil in a big saucepan on moderate heat until it starts to shimmer.
2. Put in the onion and ½ teaspoon of salt and cook until tender (approximately 5 minutes).
3. Mix the barley, garlic, and thyme and cook, stirring often, until the barley is lightly toasted and aromatic (approximately 3 minutes).
4. Mix in the water and bring to a simmer. Decrease the heat to low, cover, and simmer until the barley becomes soft and the water is absorbed (20–40 minutes).
5. Remove from the heat, and let the pilaf sit for about 10 minutes.
6. Add the parsley, chives, lemon juice, salt, and pepper to the pilaf and fluff gently with a fork to combine.
7. Serve.

Serving Suggestion: Garnish with mint leaves.
Variation Tip: Substitute fresh thyme with ½ teaspoon dried thyme.
Nutritional Information per Serving:
Calories 860 | Fat 11.1g | Sodium 39mg | Carbs 8g | Fiber 35.2g | Sugar 2.6g | Protein 22.3g

Tomato Lentil Bowl

Prep Time: 10 minutes
Cook Time: 30 minutes
Serves: 6
Ingredients:
- 2 onions, chopped
- 1 tablespoon olive oil
- 2 cups dried brown lentils, rinsed
- 4 cloves garlic, minced
- ½ teaspoon ground ginger
- 1 teaspoon salt
- ¼ teaspoon pepper
- ½ teaspoon paprika
- ¼ cup lemon juice
- 3 cups water
- ¾ cup fat-free plain Greek yogurt
- 3 tablespoons tomato paste

- Fresh cilantro, minced, optional
- Tomatoes, chopped, optional

Preparation:
1. Heat the oil over medium to high heat in a saucepan.
2. Sauté the onions for 2 minutes. Add the garlic and cook for a minute.
3. Stir in the seasonings, water, and lentils and bring to a boil. Reduce the heat.
4. Keep the saucepan covered and simmer for 25 minutes. Stir in the tomato paste and lemon juice. Heat through.
5. Serve.

Serving Suggestion: Serve with the yogurt, cilantro, and tomatoes.

Variation Tip: Substitute Greek yogurt with soy yogurt.

Nutritional Information per Serving:
Calories 294 | Fat 3g | Sodium 219mg | Carbs 49g | Fiber 8g | Sugar 5g | Protein 21g

Chickpeas with Garlic and Parsley

Prep Time: 10 Minutes
Cook Time: 20 Minutes
Serves: 6

Ingredients:
- ¼ cup extra-virgin olive oil
- 4 garlic cloves, thinly sliced
- ⅛ teaspoon red pepper flakes
- 1 onion, chopped
- Salt and pepper, to taste
- 2 (15-ounce) cans chickpeas, rinsed
- 1 cup chicken broth
- 2 tablespoons fresh parsley, minced
- 2 teaspoons lemon juice

Preparation:
1. Add three tablespoons of the oil to a skillet and cook the garlic and pepper flakes for 3 minutes over medium heat.
2. Stir in the onion and ¼ teaspoon of salt and cook for 5–7 minutes.
3. Mix in the chickpeas and broth and bring to a simmer.
4. Lower the heat and simmer on low for 7 minutes, covered.
5. Uncover and set the heat to high and cook for 3 minutes, or until all the liquid has evaporated.
6. Set aside and mix in the lemon juice and parsley.

7. Season with salt and pepper to taste and serve.

Serving Suggestion: Drizzle with a tablespoon of olive oil.

Variation Tip: Add more seasoning if required.

Nutritional Information per Serving:
Calories 611 | Fat 17.6g | Sodium 163mg | Carbs 89.5g | Fiber 25.2g | Sugar 16.1g | Protein 28.7g

Mediterranean Tomato Rice

Prep Time: 20 minutes
Cook Time: 20 minutes
Serves: 4

Ingredients:
- 2 garlic cloves, minced
- 1 cup onions, chopped
- 2 tablespoons olive oil
- 1 teaspoon dried thyme
- 1 cup green bell pepper, diced
- 1 tablespoon tomato paste
- 3 cups rice, cooked
- 1 cup celery, thinly sliced
- ½ teaspoon dried marjoram
- 1(15-ounce) can tomatoes, drained and liquid reserved
- Salt and black pepper, to taste

Preparation:
1. In a big skillet placed over medium heat, sauté the olive oil, onions, and garlic for about 5 minutes, frequently stirring.
2. Stir in the marjoram, celery, and thyme, and cook for 2 more minutes.
3. Add in the bell pepper and cook for 3 more minutes, stirring occasionally.
4. Stir in the drained tomatoes, tomato paste, salt, and black pepper.
5. Fold in the rice and stir well to mix thoroughly.
6. Dish out and serve warm.

Serving Suggestion: Serve with Mediterranean vegetable curry.

Variation Tip: You can add seasonings of your choice.

Nutritional Information per Serving:
Calories: 617 | Fat: 8.3g | Sat Fat: 1.3g | Carbohydrates: 122.3g | Fiber: 4.8g | Sugar: 6.5g | Protein: 11.9g

Grilled Lemon Salmon

Prep Time: 15 minutes
Cook Time: 12 minutes
Serves: 4
Ingredients:
- 3 garlic cloves, minced
- ½ cup plain Greek yogurt
- 2 tablespoons fresh dill, minced
- 1 tablespoon olive oil, extra-virgin
- 1½ teaspoons ground cumin
- 4 (6-ounce) salmon fillets, skinless
- 2 tablespoons fresh basil leaves
- 2 tablespoons fresh lemon juice
- 1½ teaspoons ground cilantro
- Salt and black pepper, to taste
- Olive oil cooking spray

Preparation:
1. Mix all the ingredients, except the salmon and basil, in a large bowl.
2. Move half of the mixture into another bowl and place it in the refrigerator.
3. In the large bowl of the remaining yogurt mixture, add the salmon fillets and coat well.
4. Refrigerate for about 30 minutes, flipping once halfway.
5. Preheat the broiler to medium-high heat and lightly grease a baking pan with the cooking spray.
6. Remove the salmon fillets from the bowl and discard the excess yogurt mixture.
7. Arrange the salmon fillets onto the baking pan and cook for about 6 minutes per side.
8. Remove from the broiler and place onto the serving plates.
9. Serve garnished with the basil and topped with the reserved yogurt mixture.
Serving Suggestion: Serve with roasted veggies.
Variation Tip: You can use parsley leaves instead of basil.
Nutritional Information per Serving:
Calories: 284 | Fat: 14.3g | Sat Fat: 2.1g | Carbohydrates: 3g | Fiber: 0.4g | Sugar: 1g | Protein: 36.7g

Salmon with White Sauce

Prep Time: 10 minutes
Cook Time: 25 minutes
Serves: 7
Ingredients:
- 1 teaspoon ground black pepper
- 1 tablespoon olive oil
- 1 teaspoon oregano
- 1 white onion, chopped
- 1 cup milk
- 3 garlic cloves, crushed
- 1 tablespoon pistachio, crushed
- 1 teaspoon salt
- 3 pounds salmon fillets
- 3 bay leaves
- 3 tablespoons flour
- 3 tablespoons almond butter

Preparation:
1. Rub the salmon fillets with salt, ground black pepper, and oregano, and leave for some time to marinate.
2. Meanwhile, boil the milk in a saucepan.
3. Add the chopped onion and let it simmer for 5 minutes.
4. Add the garlic cloves and bay leaf, then simmer for 4 minutes on low heat.
5. After this, remove the bay leaf from the milk, add the flour, and pulse the mixture with a blender.
6. Add the butter and leave it to get warm in the sauce. Stir the sauce from time to time to get it well-blended.
7. Pour the olive oil into a skillet and add the marinated salmon. (You may need to cook in batches, depending on the size of your skillet and the fillets.)
8. Sear the fillets on both sides for 2 minutes on high heat.
9. Add the crushed pistachio to the white sauce.
10. Take a dish, put the roasted salmon with a drizzle of the white sauce, and transfer it to the oven.
11. Cook the salmon for 15 minutes in a preheated oven at 360℉.
12. When the salmon is cooked, drizzle it with the remaining white sauce.
Serving Suggestion: Top with chopped parsley.
Variation Tip: Substitute salmon with trout.
Nutritional Information per Serving:
Calories 359 | Fat 18.9g | Sodium 440mg | Carbs 8.1g | Fiber 1.4g | Sugar 2.6g | Protein 41.1g

Greek Tilapia

Prep Time: 10 minutes
Cook Time: 18 minutes
Serves: 4
Ingredients:
- 4 tilapia fillets
- ½ cup Feta cheese, crumbled
- 2 tablespoons olive oil
- 4 tomatoes, chopped
- ½ cup parsley, chopped
- 1 tablespoon garlic, minced
- Pepper
- Salt

Directions:
1. Preheat the oven to 400° F.
2. Place fish fillets into the baking dish.
3. Drizzle with oil and season with pepper and salt.
4. Add cheese, garlic, and tomatoes on top of fish fillets.
5. Bake for 15-18 minutes.

Serving Suggestion: Garnish with parsley and serve.

Variation tip: You can also use crumbled Goat cheese instead of Feta cheese.

Nutritional Information per Serving:
Calories 231 | Fat 12.3g | Sodium 299mg | Carbs 6.7g | Fiber 1.8g | Sugar 4.1g | Protein 25.1g

Zesty Garlic Salmon

Prep Time: 10 Minutes
Cook Time: 18 Minutes
Serves: 6
Ingredients:
Salmon
- 2 pounds salmon fillet
- 2 tablespoons parsley, chopped, for garnish
- Olive oil
- Kosher salt, to taste
- ½ lemon, sliced, for garnish

Lemon-garlic sauce
- Zest of one lemon
- 3 tablespoons olive oil
- 3 tablespoons lemon juice
- 5 garlic cloves, chopped
- 1 teaspoon sweet paprika
- ½ teaspoon dry oregano
- ½ teaspoon black pepper

Preparation:
1. Preheat the oven to 375°F.
2. In a bowl, whisk the olive oil, pepper, garlic, lemon zest and juice, oregano, and paprika in a mixing bowl and set aside. The lemon-garlic sauce is ready!
3. Line a baking tray with foil and brush it with oil.
4. Season the salmon with salt and place it on the baking tray. Pour the lemon-garlic sauce over the salmon.
5. Bake in the preheated oven for 20 minutes.
6. Broil the baked salmon for 3 minutes and serve.

Serving Suggestion: Serve garnished with the fresh parsley and lemon slices.

Variation Tip: You can substitute the olive oil in the lemon-garlic sauce with other tipping sauce as you like.

Nutritional Information per Serving:
Calories 338 | Fat 25.8g | Sodium 341mg | Carbs 11.8g | Fiber 3g | Sugar 2.9g | Protein 33.1g

Clams Toscano

Prep Time: 10 minutes
Cook Time: 15 minutes
Serves: 6
Ingredients:
- 36 clams in the shell, scrubbed
- 3 tablespoons olive oil
- 5 cloves garlic, minced
- 2 cups fish broth
- 1 tablespoon dried oregano
- 1 tablespoon dried parsley
- 1 teaspoon crushed red pepper flakes (optional)

Preparation:
1. Stir fry your garlic in olive oil for a minute, then add the pepper flakes, broth, parsley, and oregano.
2. Add in the clams and stir the mix.
3. Place a lid on the pan and let everything cook until the clams open.
4. Divide the mix between serving bowls.
5. Enjoy.

Serving Suggestion: Garnish with cilantro.

Variation Tip: Substitute fish stock with chicken stock.

Nutritional Information per Serving:
Calories 227 | Fat 15.7 g | Sodium 126 mg | Carbs 4.4g | Fiber 0.5g | Sugar 0.3g | Protein 3.2 g

Easy Shrimp Skewers

Prep Time: 10 minutes
Cook Time: 10 minutes
Serves: 6
Ingredients:
1 ½ pound shrimp, deveined
1 teaspoon sweet paprika
2 fresh lemon juice
2 teaspoon garlic paste
¼ cup olive oil
½ tablespoon dried oregano
Pepper
Salt
Directions:
1. Add shrimp and remaining ingredients into the bowl and toss well.
2. Cover and place in the refrigerator for 2 hours.
3. Thread marinated shrimp onto the soaked wooden skewers.
4. Grill shrimp for 5-7 minutes. Turn halfway through.
Serving Suggestion: Garnish with chopped parsley and serve.
Variation Tip: Add ¼ teaspoon of smoked paprika for more spicy flavor.
Nutritional Information per Serving:
Calories 214 | Fat 10.5g | Sodium 307mg | Carbs 2.8g | Fiber 0.4g | Sugar 0.4g | Protein 26.1g

Healthy Shrimp Egg Salad

Prep Time: 10 minutes
Cook Time: 10 minutes
Serves: 4
Ingredients:

2 eggs, hard-boiled and chopped
1 pound medium shrimp, peeled, deveined, and cooked
4 tablespoons mayonnaise
½ green bell pepper, chopped
2 celery stalks, diced
½ onion, diced
2 tablespoons fresh lime juice
1 Jalapeno pepper, chopped
2 radishes, diced
Salt
Directions:
1. Add shrimp and remaining ingredients into the bowl and mix well.
Serving Suggestion: Garnish with parsley and serve.
Variation Tip: Add your choice of salad dressing.
Nutritional Information per Serving:
Calories 215 | Fat 8.5g | Sodium 440mg | Carbs 8.5g | Fiber 0.9g | Sugar 3.1g | Protein 27.7g

Herb-Crusted Halibut

Prep Time: 10 Minutes
Cook Time: 15 Minutes
Serves: 4
Ingredients:
- ⅓ cup fresh parsley
- ¼ cup fresh dill
- ¼ cup fresh chives
- 1 teaspoon lemon zest
- ¾ cup panko breadcrumbs
- 1 tablespoon olive oil
- ¼ teaspoon freshly cracked black pepper
- 1 teaspoon sea salt
- 4–6 ounces halibut fillets
Preparation:
1. Chop the fresh dill, chives, and parsley.
2. Line a baking tray with foil. Set the oven to 400°F.
3. Combine the salt, pepper, lemon zest, olive oil, chives, dill, parsley, and breadcrumbs in a mixing bowl.
4. Rinse the halibut thoroughly. Use paper towels to dry it before baking. Arrange the fish on the baking sheet.
5. Spoon the crumbs over the fish and press them into each of the fillets.
6. Bake until the top is browned and easily flaked (about 10–15 minutes).
Serving Suggestion: Serve with savory potatoes and peas.
Variation Tip: You can use other fresh herbs of your liking.
Nutritional Information per Serving:
Calories 273 | Fat 7g | Sodium 593mg | Carbs 5.1g | Fiber 1.1g | Sugar 0.2g | Protein 38g

Halibut with Kale

Prep Time: 10 minutes
Cook Time: 15 minutes
Serves: 4
Ingredients:
• 3 tablespoons olive oil, divided
• 3 cups kale, coarsely chopped
• 2 cups cherry tomatoes, halved
• 4 (4-ounce) boneless, skinless halibut fillets
• Juice and zest of 1 lemon
• Sea salt and black pepper, to taste
• 1 tablespoon fresh basil, chopped
Preparation:
1. Preheat the oven to 375°F.
2. Lightly grease an 8-inch x 8-inch baking dish with two teaspoons of olive oil.
3. Arrange the kale in the bottom of the baking dish and top with the cherry tomatoes and the halibut.
4. Drizzle over the remaining olive oil and the lemon juice, lemon zest, basil, salt, and pepper.
5. Bake until the fish flakes easily and the greens are wilted (about 15 minutes).
6. Serve and enjoy.
Serving Suggestion: Garnish with cilantro.
Variation Tip: You can also cook the fish and vegetables in individual foil packets on a baking sheet instead of in a baking dish for easy serving.
Nutritional Information per Serving:
Calories 228 | Fat 10g | Sodium 284mg | Carbs 9g | Fiber 2g | Sugar 2g | Protein 28g

Zesty Scallops

Prep Time: 10 minutes
Cook Time: 5 minutes
Serves: 4
Ingredients:
• 1-pound sea scallops
• Sea salt and black pepper, to taste
• 2 tablespoons olive oil
• Juice of 1 lime
• Pinch of red pepper flakes

• 1 tablespoon fresh cilantro, chopped
Preparation:
1. Season the scallops lightly with salt and pepper.
2. In a large skillet, heat the olive oil over medium-high heat.
3. Add the scallops to the skillet, making sure they don't touch one another.
4. Sear on both sides, turning once, for a total of about 3 minutes.
5. Add the lime juice and red pepper flakes to the skillet and toss the scallops in the juice.
6. Serve.
Serving Suggestion: Top with the fresh cilantro.
Variation Tip: Look for dried scallops not stored in a milky liquid called sodium triphosphate. This additive causes the scallops to soak up water, and your scallops will have less flavor.
Nutritional Information per Serving:
Calories 160 | Fat 8g | Sodium 241mg | Carbs 3g | Fiber 0.1g | Sugar 0.2g | Protein 19g

Baked Trout With Dill

Prep Time: 10 minutes
Cook Time: 20 minutes
Serves: 4
Ingredients:
• 3 teaspoons olive oil, divided
• 2 (8-ounce) whole trout, cleaned
• Sea salt and black pepper, to taste
• 1 lemon, thinly sliced into about 6 pieces
• 1 tablespoon fresh dill, finely chopped
• 1 tablespoon fresh parsley, chopped
• ½ cup low-sodium fish stock
Preparation:
1. Preheat the oven to 400°F.
2. Lightly grease a 9-inch x 13-inch baking dish with one teaspoon of olive oil.
3. Rinse the trout, pat dry with paper towels, and coat with the remaining two teaspoons of olive oil. Season with salt and pepper.
4. Stuff the interior of the trout with the lemon slices, dill, and parsley and place it into the prepared baking dish.
5. Bake the fish for 10 minutes, then add the fish stock to the dish.
6. Continue to bake until the fish flakes easily with a fork, about 10 minutes.
7. Serve.
Serving Suggestion: Garnish with fresh dill and lemon slices.
Variation Tip: Substitute fish stock with chicken stock.
Nutritional Information per Serving:
Calories 194 | Fat 10g | Sodium 128mg | Carbs 1g | Fiber 0g | Sugar 0g | Protein 25g

Greek Stuffed Squid

Prep Time: 10 minutes
Cook Time: 1 hour 15 minutes
Serves: 4

Ingredients:
- ¼ cup golden raisins
- ¼ cup pine nuts, toasted
- ½ cup red wine
- ½ cup plain dried breadcrumbs
- 1 (15-ounce) can tomato sauce
- 1 garlic clove, minced
- 1 tablespoon dried mint
- 16 medium squid bodies, plus 6 ounces tentacles, chopped
- 2 tablespoons extra-virgin olive oil
- 3 onions, finely chopped
- 4 anchovy fillets, rinsed and minced
- 5 tablespoons fresh parsley, minced
- Salt and pepper, to taste

Preparation:
1. Heat 1 tablespoon of oil in a 12-inch non-stick frying pan on moderate to high heat until it starts to shimmer.
2. Put in two-thirds of the onions and cook until they become tender (approximately 5 minutes). Mix in squid tentacles and cook until no longer translucent, 1–2 minutes.
3. Mix in the pine nuts, mint, and ¼ teaspoon pepper and cook until aromatic, approximately 1 minute.
4. Move the mixture to a large bowl and mix in the breadcrumbs, ¼ cup parsley, raisins, and anchovies.
5. Sprinkle with salt and pepper to taste and allow to cool slightly.
6. Using a small soup spoon, portion 2 tablespoons of filling into each squid body, pressing on the filling gently to create a 1-inch space at the top.
7. Thread a toothpick through the opening of each squid to close securely.
8. Heat the residual 1 tablespoon of oil in the now-empty frying pan on moderate to high heat until it starts to shimmer.
9. Put in the remaining onions and cook until they become tender (approximately 5 minutes).
10. Mix in the garlic, ¼ teaspoon salt, and ¼ teaspoon pepper and cook until aromatic, approximately half a minute.
11. Mix in the wine, tomato sauce, salt, and pepper and bring to simmer.
12. Add the squid into the sauce.
13. Reduce the heat to low, cover, and simmer gently until the sauce has thickened slightly and the squid is easily pierced with a paring knife, about 1 hour, turning the squid halfway through cooking.
14. Season the sauce with salt and pepper to taste.

15. Remove the toothpicks from the squid and garnish with the remaining 1 tablespoon of parsley.
16. Serve.

Serving Suggestion: Garnish with basil leaves.
Variation Tip: Add chili for a kick.
Nutritional Information per Serving:
Calories 733 | Fat 22.3g | Sodium 1012mg | Carbs 44.9g | Fiber 4.9g | Sugar 14.8g | Protein 55g

Classic Calamari Stew

Prep Time: 10 minutes
Cook Time: 45 minutes
Serves: 6

Ingredients:
- ¼ cup extra-virgin olive oil, plus extra for serving
- ¼ teaspoon red pepper flakes
- ⅓ cup pitted brine-cured green olives, coarsely chopped
- ½ cup red wine
- 1 tablespoon capers, rinsed
- 2 celery ribs, thinly sliced
- 2 onions, finely chopped
- 2 pounds small squid, bodies sliced crosswise into 1-inch-thick rings, tentacles halved
- 3 (28-ounce) cans whole peeled tomatoes, drained and chopped coarsely
- 3 tablespoons fresh parsley, minced
- 8 garlic cloves, minced
- Salt and pepper, to taste

Preparation:
1. Heat the oil in a Dutch oven on moderate to high heat until it starts to shimmer.
2. Put in the onions and celery and cook until they become tender (approximately 5 minutes).
3. Mix in the garlic and pepper flakes and cook until aromatic, approximately half a minute.
4. Mix in the wine, and cook until nearly evaporated (approximately 1 minute).
5. Pat the squid dry using paper towels and sprinkle with salt and pepper. Stir the squid into the pot.
6. Reduce the heat to moderate to low, cover, and simmer gently until the squid has released its liquid (about 15 minutes).
7. Mix in the tomatoes, olives, and capers, cover, and continue cooking until the squid is very tender (30 minutes).
8. Remove from the heat, mix in the parsley and sprinkle with salt and pepper to taste.

Serving Suggestion: Serve, drizzling individual portions with extra oil.
Variation Tip: Add chili for a hotter flavor.
Nutritional Information per Serving:
Calories 480 | Fat 13.3g | Sodium 217mg | Carbs 32g | Fiber 3.8g | Sugar 1.9g | Protein 26.7g

Octopus Braised in Red Wine

Prep Time: 10 minutes
Cook Time: 2 hours
Serves: 4

Ingredients:
- 1 (4-pound) octopus, rinsed
- 1 cup dry red wine
- 1 sprig of fresh rosemary
- 1 tablespoon extra-virgin olive oil
- 2 bay leaves
- 2 tablespoons red wine vinegar
- 2 tablespoons tomato paste
- 2 tablespoons unflavored gelatin
- 2 teaspoons fresh parsley, chopped
- 4 garlic cloves, peeled and smashed
- Salt and black pepper, to taste
- Pinch of ground cinnamon
- Pinch of ground nutmeg

Preparation:
1. Using a sharp knife, separate the octopus mantle (large sac) and body (lower section with tentacles) from the head (midsection containing eyes); discard the head.
2. Place the octopus in a large pot, cover with water by 2 inches, and bring to a simmer on high heat.
3. Reduce the heat, cover, and simmer gently, flipping the octopus occasionally, until the skin between the tentacle joints tears easily when pulled (45 minutes to 1¼ hours).
4. Move the octopus to a slicing board and allow it to cool slightly.
5. Measure out and reserve 3 cups of the octopus cooking liquid; discard the remaining liquid and wipe the pot dry using paper towels.
6. While the octopus is still warm, use a paring knife to cut the mantle into quarters, trimming and scraping away skin and interior fibers. Transfer it to a bowl. Using your fingers, remove the skin from the body, being careful not to remove the suction cups from the tentacles. Cut the tentacles from around the core of the body in three sections; discard the core.
7. Separate the tentacles and cut them into 2-inch lengths; move to a bowl.
8. Heat the oil in the now-empty pot on moderate to high heat until it starts to shimmer.
9. Put in the tomato paste and cook, stirring continuously, until starting to darken, approximately 1 minute.
10. Mix in the garlic, rosemary sprig, bay leaves, ½ teaspoon pepper, cinnamon, and nutmeg, and cook until aromatic, approximately half a minute.
11. Mix in the reserved octopus cooking liquid, wine, vinegar, and gelatin, scraping up any browned bits. Bring to a boil and cook, stirring intermittently, for 20 minutes.
12. Mix in the octopus and any accumulated juices and bring to a simmer.

13. Cook, stirring intermittently, until the octopus becomes soft and the sauce has thickened slightly and coats the back of a spoon (20 minutes to half an hour).
14. Remove from the heat and discard the rosemary sprig and bay leaves.
15. Serve.

Serving Suggestion: Mix in parsley and season with pepper to taste.

Variation Tip: Add a tablespoon of paprika for a more vibrant dish.

Nutritional Information per Serving:
Calories 457 | Fat 7.9g | Sodium 22mg | Carbs 5.2g | Fiber 0.8g | Sugar 1.5g | Protein 75g

Octopus in Honey Sauce

Prep Time: 20 minutes
Cook Time: 1 hour 25 minutes
Serves: 8

Ingredients:
- 1 bay leaf
- 2¼ pounds fresh octopus, washed
- ⅓ cup water
- 2 onions, finely chopped
- 1 garlic clove, finely chopped
- 1 (14-ounce) can diced low-sodium tomatoes
- ¾ cup red wine
- ¼ cup fresh basil leaves, chopped
- 4 tablespoons olive oil
- 1 pinch saffron thread, crushed
- 1 tablespoon tomato paste
- 1 tablespoon honey
- Salt and black pepper, to taste

Preparation:
1. Prepare and clean the head of the octopus.
2. In a heavy-bottomed pan placed over medium heat, add the octopus, bay leaf, and water, and cook for about 20 minutes.
3. Stir in the wine and simmer for about 50 minutes.
4. For the sauce: In a skillet placed over medium heat, heat the olive oil and sauté the onions and saffron for about 4 minutes.
5. Stir in the tomato paste and garlic and sauté for about 2 minutes.
6. Stir in the tomatoes and honey and simmer for about 10 minutes.
7. Transfer the sauce into the pan with the octopus and cook for about 15 minutes.
8. Serve hot garnished with the basil.

Serving Suggestion: Serve with egg noodles on the side.

Variation Tip: Saffron threads can be omitted if not available.

Nutritional Information per Serving:
Calories: 319 | Fat: 10.2g | Sat Fat: 1g | Carbohydrates: 13.9g | Fiber: 1.3g | Sugar: 5g | Protein: 38.4g

Baked Mackerel

Prep Time: 10 minutes
Cook Time: 20 minutes
Serves: 6
Ingredients:
- 2 tablespoons lemon juice
- 2 pounds mackerel fillets
- 1 teaspoon salt
- 3 tablespoons olive oil
- ⅛ teaspoon paprika
- ⅛ teaspoon black pepper

Preparation:
1. Preheat the oven to 350°F.
2. Mix all the items in a bowl except the fillets.
3. Coat the fillets with the mixture, place them in a baking dish, and bake for 25 minutes.
Serving Suggestion: Serve with baked potatoes.
Variation Tip: Substitute mackerel fillets with herring fillets.
Nutritional Information per Serving:
Calories 399 | Fat 31g | Sodium 514mg | Carbs 0.5g | Fiber 0.2g | Sugar 0.2g | Protein 28.8g

Mahi-Mahi and Mushrooms

Prep Time: 10 minutes
Cook Time: 25 minutes
Serves: 4
Ingredients:
- 3 tablespoons olive oil, divided
- ¼ cup lemon juice
- ¼ cup fresh chives, minced
- ¼ cup pine nuts or nuts of your choice
- 1 large onion, chopped
- 5 pounds portobello mushrooms, chopped
- Salt and black pepper, to taste
- ¾ cup bell pepper, chopped
- 4 (6 ounces) mahi-mahi fillets

Preparation:
1. In a large skillet on medium heat, lightly fry the fish for 8 minutes in olive oil until the fish begins to flake. Remove from the heat.

2. Add the bell peppers, onions, lemon juice, and mushrooms into the remaining oil. Season with salt and pepper. Cook until the peppers are tender.
3. Add the fish on top and season the fillets with salt and black pepper.
4. Cook for a bit longer until the fish is cooked through.
Serving Suggestion: Garnish with toasted pine nuts and chives before serving.
Variation Tip: You can substitute mahi-mahi with salmon.
Nutritional Information per Serving:
Calories 444 | Fat 16.6g | Sodium 148mg | Carbs 27g | Fiber 8.3g | Sugar 3.4g | Protein 53.9g

Almond-Crusted Tilapia

Prep Time: 15 minutes
Cook Time: 10 minutes
Serves: 4
Ingredients:
- ¼ cup ground flax seeds
- 1 cup almonds, finely chopped and divided
- 4 (6-ounce) tilapia fillets
- 2 tablespoons olive oil
- Salt and black pepper, to taste

Preparation:
1. Mix half a cup of the almonds with the ground flax seeds in a large shallow dish.
2. Season the tilapia fillets with salt and black pepper.
3. Rub the tilapia fillets in the almond mixture and coat evenly.
4. In a heavy skillet placed over medium heat, heat the oil and cook the tilapia fillets for about 4 minutes per side.
5. Put the tilapia fillets onto a serving plate.
6. In the same heavy skillet, add the remaining almonds and cook for about 1 minute, frequently stirring.
7. Remove the almonds from the heat and sprinkle over the fish.
8. Serve warm.
Serving Suggestion: Top with sprigs of rosemary and lemon wedges.
Variation Tip: You can also add peanuts.
Nutritional Information per Serving:
Calories: 374 | Fat: 22.6g | Sat Fat: 2.9g | Carbohydrates: 7.1g | Fiber: 4.9g | Sugar: 1.1g | Protein: 38g

Citrus Scallops

Prep Time: 10 minutes
Cook Time: 18 minutes
Serves: 4
Ingredients:
- 1 sweet pepper, sliced
- 1 pound sea scallops
- 5 green onions, chopped
- Salt and black pepper, to taste
- 3 tablespoons olive oil
- ¼ teaspoon red pepper flakes
- 4 medium oranges, peeled and sectioned
- 2 teaspoons fresh cilantro or parsley, diced
- 3 tablespoons lime juice
- 4 cloves garlic, minced

Preparation:
1. In a large skillet, lightly fry the onions, garlic, and pepper in olive oil until the vegetables are soft.
2. Add the scallops and sprinkle with pepper, black pepper, and salt. Cook until the scallops are cooked through. Add the lime juice.
3. Reduce the heat before adding the orange slices and fresh cilantro.
4. Cook until the scallops are lightly golden.
5. Remove from the heat and serve.
Serving Suggestion: Garnish with parsley.
Variation Tip: Switch up oranges with clementine or grapefruit.
Nutritional Information per Serving:
Calories 275 | Fat 11.7g | Sodium 187mg | Carbs 23.7g | Fiber 4.2g | Sugar 14.4g | Protein 21.1g

Cheesy Tilapia

Prep Time: 10 minutes
Cook Time: 15 minutes
Serves: 7
Ingredients:
- ¼ cup flour
- 1 tablespoon olive oil
- 1 teaspoon dried dill
- 2 pounds tilapia fillet
- 7 ounces parmesan cheese, grated

- 1 tablespoon paprika
- 1 teaspoon dried oregano

Preparation:
1. Combine the paprika, dried dill, dried oregano, and flour. Mix well.
2. Pour the olive oil into a skillet and heat over medium heat.
3. Rub the tilapia fillets with the oregano mixture.
4. Sear the tilapia for 10 minutes in the skillet on both sides.
5. Sprinkle the grated cheese over the fish and cover it with a lid.
6. Cook the tilapia for 2 minutes more.
7. Serve hot!
Serving Suggestion: Serve with your favorite greens.
Variation Tip: Add in chili for a hotter taste.
Nutritional Information per Serving:
Calories 235 | Fat 9.4g | Sodium 310mg | Carbs 5.2g | Fiber 0.6g | Sugar 0.1g | Protein 33.9g

Grilled Salmon

Prep Time: 10 minutes
Cook Time: 27 minutes
Serves: 6
Ingredients:
- 1½ pounds salmon fillet
- 1 tablespoon garlic powder
- ⅓ cup soy sauce
- ⅓ cup brown sugar
- ⅓ cup water
- ¼ cup olive oil
- Salt and pepper, to taste
- 1 lemon, juiced

Preparation:
1. Season the salmon fillets with lemon, pepper, salt, and garlic powder.
2. Mix the soy sauce, brown sugar, water, and olive oil in a small bowl until the sugar is dissolved.
3. Place the fish in a big resealable plastic bag with the soy sauce mixture, seal, and let marinate for at least 2 hours.
4. Preheat the broiler on medium heat. Lightly oil a griddle pan.
5. Set the salmon on the pan and discard the marinade.
6. Broil the salmon for 7 minutes per side or until the fish flakes easily with a fork.
Serving Suggestion: Serve with some greens.
Variation Tip: Add chili for extra heat.
Nutritional Information per Serving:
Calories 318| Fat 20.1g | Sodium 987mg | Carbs 13.2g | Fiber 3g | Sugar 1.9g | Protein 20.5g

Lamb Chops with Veggies

Prep Time: 20 minutes (plus 3 hours for marinating)
Cook Time: 27 minutes
Serves: 4

Ingredients:
- ½ cup fresh basil leaves
- 8 (4-ounce) lamb loin chops
- ½ cup fresh mint leaves
- 2 garlic cloves
- 2 zucchinis, sliced
- 1 eggplant, sliced
- 8 ounces fresh cherry tomatoes
- 1 tablespoon fresh rosemary leaves
- 3 tablespoons olive oil
- 1 red bell pepper, seeded and chunked
- 1¾ ounces feta cheese, crumbled

Preparation:
1. Preheat the oven to 390°F and lightly grease a large baking sheet.
2. Process the fresh herbs, garlic, and 2 tablespoons of the olive oil in a food processor until smooth.
3. Transfer the herb mixture to a large bowl.
4. Add the lamb chops to the bowl and coat generously with the herb mixture.
5. Refrigerate to marinate for about 3 hours.
6. Arrange the zucchini, eggplant, and bell pepper on a baking sheet and drizzle with the remaining olive oil.
7. Top with the lamb chops in a single layer and bake for about 20 minutes.
8. Remove the chops and place them on a platter. Wrap the chops with foil to keep them warm.
9. Top the veggies on the baking sheet with the feta cheese.
10. Bake for another 7 minutes and transfer to a platter for serving.

Serving Suggestion: Serve with a dip of your choice.
Variation Tip: Parsley leaves can be added.
Nutritional Information per Serving:
Calories: 619 | Fat: 30.6g | Sat Fat: 9.4g | Carbohydrates: 17.1g | Fiber: 7.4g | Sugar: 8.7g | Protein: 69.2 g

Beef Kebabs

Prep Time: 10 minutes plus 12 hours marinating time
Cook Time: 15 minutes
Serves: 10

Ingredients:
- 4 pounds beef sirloin, cut into cubes
- 2 onions, quartered
- 1 large bell pepper, cut into large cubes
- 5 small tomatoes, halved
- 1 tablespoon olive oil
- Salt and pepper, to taste

To serve:
- Slices of thick, crusty bread (optional)

For the marinade:
- 8 cloves garlic, minced or pounded into a paste
- 4 bay leaves, crumbled
- ¾ cup red wine of choice
- 3 tablespoons olive oil

Preparation:
1. Combine the marinade ingredients and pour into a shallow dish or Ziploc bag. Add the beef cubes and let marinate overnight.
2. Skewer the beef, alternating with the onion, bell pepper, and tomato. If using bamboo skewers, soak them in water for 1 hour before using.
3. Brush with olive oil and season with salt and pepper.
4. Cook on a grill pan (at medium heat) or broil. Cooking time depends on desired doneness (about 8 to 15 minutes).
5. Serve.

Serving Suggestion: Lay on slices of bread.
Variation Tip: Substitute beef with lamb.
Nutritional Information per Serving:
Calories 451 | Fat 19.6g | Sodium 370mg | Carbs 5.1g | Fiber 1.2g | Sugar 2.7g | Protein 55.4g

Pork Skewers

Prep Time: 10 minutes
Cook Time: 8 minutes
Serves: 6
Ingredients:
2 pounds pork tenderloin, cut into 1-inch cubes
½ cup olive oil
½ cup vinegar
3 tablespoons fresh parsley, chopped
1 tablespoon garlic, chopped
1 onion, chopped
Pepper
Salt
Directions:
1. Add meat and remaining ingredients into the zip-lock bag, seal bag and place in refrigerator for overnight.
2. Thread marinated meat pieces onto soaked wooden skewers.
3. Preheat the grill.
4. Place meat skewers onto the grill and cook for 4 minutes on each side.
Serving Suggestion: Garnish with parsley and serve.
Variation Tip: Add your choice of seasonings.
Nutritional Information per Serving:
Calories 375 | Fat 22.2g | Sodium 116mg | Carbs 2.5g | Fiber 0.5g | Sugar 0.9g | Protein 39.9g

Lamb Stew

Prep Time: 10 minutes
Cook Time: 30 minutes
Serves: 4
Ingredients:

2 pounds lamb, cut into chunks
1 teaspoon dried oregano
1 tablespoon olive oil
1 tablespoon garlic, minced
1 cup tomatoes, chopped
1 cup olives, pitted and sliced
1 onion, chopped
½ cup cilantro, chopped
Pepper
Salt
Directions:
1. Add oil into the instant pot and set pot on sauté mode.
2. Add onion, garlic and oregano and cook for 5 minutes.
3. Add meat and sauté for 5 minutes.
4. Add remaining ingredients and stir well.
5. Cover and cook on high for 20 minutes.
6. Once done, allow to release pressure naturally. Remove the lid.
Serving Suggestion: Garnish with cilantro and serve.
Variation Tip: Top with crumbled cheese.
Nutritional Information per Serving:
Calories 514 | Fat 23.9g | Sodium 204mg | Carbs 7.4g | Fiber 2.5g | Sugar 2.4g | Protein 64.9g

Roasted Pepper Artichoke Beef

Prep Time: 10 minutes
Cook Time: 6 hours
Serves: 6
Ingredients:
2 pounds stew beef, cut into 1-inch cubes
12 ounces roasted red peppers, drained and sliced
12 ounces artichoke hearts, drained
1 teaspoon dried basil
1 teaspoon dried oregano
1 onion, diced
1 ½ cups Marinara sauce
Directions:
1. Add all meat and remaining ingredients into the slow cooker and stir well.
2. Cover and cook on low for 6 hours.
Serving Suggestion: Allow to cool slightly and serve.
Variation Tip: Add ¼ cup of freshly chopped parsley.
Nutritional Information per Serving:
Calories 325 | Fat 11g | Sodium 445mg | Carbs 19.9g | Fiber 5.9g | Sugar 9.4g | Protein 37g

Roasted Pork Tenderloin

Prep Time: 1 hour 10 minutes
Cook Time: 20 minutes
Serves: 4

Ingredients:
* ¼ cup olive oil
* ¼ cup fresh rosemary, chopped
* Juice of 1 lemon
* Juice and zest of 1 lime
* 1 teaspoon garlic, minced
* 1 teaspoon ground cumin
* Sea salt, to taste
* 12 ounces boneless pork tenderloin

Preparation:
1. Whisk the salt, olive oil, rosemary, lemon juice, lime juice, lime zest, garlic, and cumin in a medium bowl.
2. Add the pork tenderloin to the bowl, and coat thoroughly. Cover and refrigerate for 1 hour.
3. Preheat a grill to medium-high heat.
4. Grill the tenderloin, turning several times and basting with the remaining marinade until it is cooked through (internal temperature: 140°F), 20 minutes.
5. Remove the tenderloin from the grill, cover it with foil, and let rest for 10 minutes.
6. Serve.
Serving Suggestion: Garnish with cilantro sprigs.
Variation Tip: Alternatively, roast the tenderloin on a baking sheet in a 400°F oven until cooked through, 25–30 minutes.
Nutritional Information per Serving:
Calories 201 | Fat 15g | Sodium 81mg | Carbs 1g | Fiber 0.1 g | Sugar 0.2g | Protein 20g

Sriracha Lamb Chops

Prep Time: 10 minutes
Cook Time: 10 minutes
Serves: 4

Ingredients:
* 4 (4-ounce) loin lamb chops with bones, trimmed
* Sea salt and black pepper, to taste
* 1 tablespoon olive oil
* 2 tablespoons sriracha sauce
* 1 tablespoon fresh cilantro, chopped

Preparation:
1. Preheat the oven to 450°F.
2. Lightly season the lamb chops with salt and pepper.
3. In a large ovenproof skillet, heat the olive oil over medium-high heat.
4. Brown the chops on both sides, about 2 minutes per side, and then spread the chops with sriracha.
5. Place the skillet in the oven and roast until the desired doneness, 4–5 minutes for medium.
6. Serve.
Serving Suggestion: Top with cilantro.
Variation Tip: Use pork tenderloin or chicken instead of lamb, in the same amount.
Nutritional Information per Serving:
Calories 223 | Fat 14g | Sodium 116mg | Carbs 1g | Fiber 0g | Sugar 1g | Protein 23g

Thyme Lamb

Prep Time: 10 minutes
Cook Time: 20 minutes
Serves: 2

Ingredients:
* 8 ounces lamb shanks
* 1 tablespoon thyme
* 1 teaspoon garlic, minced
* 1 tablespoon balsamic vinegar
* Salt and black pepper, to taste
* 1 tablespoon olive oil
* ½ cup water
* 1 tablespoon fresh dill, chopped

Preparation:
1. Rub the lamb shanks with thyme, minced garlic, balsamic vinegar, salt, and ground black pepper.
2. Sprinkle the meat with olive oil and leave for 15 minutes to marinate.
3. Transfer the marinated lamb to an Instant Pot or pressure cooker and add the fresh dill.
4. Add the water and close the lid.
5. Cook for 20 minutes on high pressure.
6. Do a natural pressure release and transfer the meat to a platter.
7. Serve and enjoy!
Serving Suggestion: Garnish with fresh rosemary.
Variation Tip: Switch up lamb shanks with lamb shoulder.
Nutritional Information per Serving:
Calories 284 | Fat 15.5g | Sodium 93mg | Carbs 2.6g | Fiber 0.9g | Sugar 0.1g | Protein 32.4g

Easy Beef Roast

Prep Time: 10 minutes
Cook Time: 35 minutes
Serves: 2

Ingredients:
- 1½ teaspoons rosemary
- ½ teaspoon garlic, minced
- 2 pounds roast beef
- ⅓ cup soy sauce
- Salt, to taste

Preparation:
1. Combine the soy sauce, salt, rosemary, and garlic in a mixing bowl.
2. Place the roast in an Instant Pot or pressure cooker. Pour enough water to cover it, and then add the soy sauce mixture on top; gently stir to mix well and seal the lid.
3. Cook on high pressure for 35 minutes.
4. Allow for natural pressure release. Carefully open the lid, and shred the meat.
5. Serve warm.

Serving Suggestion: Serve with a simple salad.
Variation Tip: Add chili for heat.
Nutritional Information per Serving:
Calories 423 | Fat 14g | Sodium 884mg | Carbs 12g | Fiber 0.7g | Sugar 0.7g | Protein 21g

Baked Lamb Patties

Prep Time: 10 minutes
Cook Time: 15 minutes
Serves: 4

Ingredients:
1 pound ground lamb
1 teaspoon cinnamon
1 teaspoon coriander
1 tablespoon garlic, minced
¼ teaspoon pepper
1 teaspoon ground cumin
¼ cup fresh parsley, chopped

¼ cup onion, minced
¼ teaspoon Cayenne
½ teaspoon allspice
1 teaspoon Kosher salt

Directions:
1. Preheat the oven to 450° F.
2. Add ground meat and remaining ingredients into the bowl and mix until well combined.
3. Make patties from the meat mixture and place onto the baking sheet.
4. Bake for 12-15 minutes.

Serving Suggestion: Serve with your choice of dip.
Variation Tip: Add your choice of seasonings.
Nutritional Information per Serving:
Calories 223 | Fat 8.5g | Sodium 672mg | Carbs 2.6g | Fiber 0.8g | Sugar 0.4g | Protein 32.3g

Lamb Kofta

Prep Time: 20 minutes
Cook Time: 10 minutes
Serves: 6

Ingredients:
- 2 tablespoons fat-free plain Greek yogurt
- 1 pound ground lamb
- 2 tablespoons onion, grated
- 2 tablespoons fresh cilantro, minced
- 1 teaspoon ground cumin
- Salt and black pepper, to taste
- 2 teaspoons garlic, minced
- 1 teaspoon ground cilantro
- 1 teaspoon ground turmeric
- 1 tablespoon olive oil

Preparation:
1. Combine all the ingredients in a large bowl and mix well.
2. Make 12 equal-sized oblong patties out of the mixture.
3. Heat the olive oil in a large non-stick skillet placed over medium-high heat.
4. Add the patties and cook for about 10 minutes until browned on both sides, flipping occasionally.
5. Dish out and serve.

Serving Suggestion: Serve the koftas with yogurt sauce.
Variation Tip: You can add red chili powder for spice.
Nutritional Information per Serving:
Calories: 169 | Fat: 8g | Sat Fat: 2.3g | Carbohydrates: 1.2g | Fiber: 0.2g | Sugar: 0.3g | Protein: 21.9g

Pork and Peas

Prep Time: 10 Minutes
Cook Time: 20 Minutes
Serves: 4
Ingredients:
- 4 ounces snow peas
- 2 tablespoons avocado oil
- 1-pound boneless pork loin, cubed
- ¾ cup beef stock
- ½ cup red onion, chopped
- Salt and white pepper, to taste

Preparation:
1. Heat a pan with the oil over medium-high heat. Add the pork and brown for 5 minutes.
2. Add the peas and the rest of the ingredients, toss, bring to a simmer and cook over medium heat for 15 minutes.
3. Divide between plates and serve right away.
Serving Suggestion: Serve with mashed potatoes.
Variation Tip: You can use green onions instead.
Nutritional Information per Serving:
Calories 332 | Fat 16.5g | Sodium 219mg | Carbs 20.7g | Fiber 10.3g | Sugar 1.8g | Protein 26.5g

Garlic Veal

Prep Time: 10 minutes
Cook Time: 50 minutes
Serves: 6
Ingredients:
- 6 garlic cloves, crushed
- 3 pounds veal, cubed
- 1 cup of broth
- 1 glass of wine
- A handful of chives and parsley
- Sea salt, to taste
- Ground black pepper, to taste
- 3 tablespoons sour cream
- 4 tablespoons olive oil

Preparation:
1. Sear the veal cubes for several minutes in olive oil while constantly stirring until brown.

2. Add some chives and parsley, then sauté for several minutes.
3. Add salt and pepper as desired.
4. Add the cup of broth.
5. Slowly cook until the meat becomes tender. Add more broth as needed.
6. When the meat is tender and cooked through, add the sour cream and a glass of wine, then cook for 5 more minutes.
7. Serve.
Serving Suggestion: Garnish with basil.
Variation Tip: You can use vegetable, beef, or chicken broth.
Nutritional Information per Serving:
Calories 508 | Fat 27.9g | Sodium 399mg | Carbs 1.9g | Fiber 0.1g | Sugar 0.3g | Protein 56.4g

Almond-Crusted Rack of Lamb

Prep Time: 10 Minutes
Cook Time: 35 Minutes
Serves: 2
Ingredients:
- 2 garlic cloves, minced
- ½ tablespoon olive oil
- Salt and black pepper, to taste
- ¾ pound rack of lamb
- 1 small organic egg
- 1 tablespoon breadcrumbs
- 2 ounces almonds, finely chopped
- ½ tablespoon fresh rosemary, chopped

Preparation:
1. Preheat the oven to 350°F.
2. Meanwhile, take a baking tray, grease it with oil, and set it aside.
3. Mix the garlic, oil, salt, and freshly cracked black pepper in a bowl. Coat the rack of lamb with this mixture, rubbing it on all sides.
4. Crack the egg in a bowl, whisk it until blended, and set aside until required.
5. Place the breadcrumbs in another dish, add the almonds and rosemary and stir until mixed.
6. Dip the seasoned rack of lamb into the egg, dredge with the breadcrumbs mixture until evenly coated on all sides, and then place it onto the prepared baking tray.
7. Cook in the preheated oven for 35 minutes until thoroughly cooked.
8. When done, transfer the rack of lamb onto a dish, and serve straight away.
Serving Suggestion: Serve with a side of asparagus.
Variation Tip: Add chili if desired.
Nutritional Information per Serving:
Calories 471 | Fat 31.6g | Sodium 145mg | Carbs 8.5g | Fiber 3.1g | Sugar 1.5g | Protein 39g

Grilled Paprika Lamb Chops

Prep Time: 10 minutes
Cook Time: 15 minutes
Serves: 4

Ingredients:
- 2 lamb racks, cut into chops
- Salt and black pepper, to taste
- 3 tablespoons paprika
- ¾ cup cumin powder
- 1 teaspoon chili powder

Preparation:
1. Combine the paprika, cumin, chili, salt, pepper in a bowl.
2. Add the lamb chops and rub the mixture over them.
3. Heat a grill pan over medium heat, add the lamb chops, cook for 5 minutes.
4. Flip and cook for 5 minutes more; flip again.
5. Cook for 2 minutes, flip and cook for 2 minutes more.
6. Serve and enjoy.

Serving Suggestion: Serve with rosemary sprigs.
Variation Tip: For a milder taste, omit the chili powder.
Nutritional Information per Serving:
Calories 392 | Fat 17g | Sodium 164mg | Carbs 11.6g | Fiber 4.2g | Sugar 1g | Protein 32.1g

Parmesan Pork Chops

Prep Time: 10 minutes
Cook Time: 15 minutes
Serves: 6

Ingredients:
- 1 tablespoon salt
- 1 teaspoon ground black pepper
- 1 teaspoon chili flakes
- 2 pounds pork loin
- 1 cup breadcrumbs
- 2 tablespoons Italian seasoning
- 3 tablespoons olive oil
- 5 ounces parmesan, grated

Preparation:

1. Slice the pork loin into the serving chops. Then rub the pork chops with salt and ground black pepper.
2. Add chili flakes.
3. Combine the breadcrumbs with the Italian seasoning and stir the mixture with the help of the fork. Add the grated parmesan and stir.
4. Pour the olive oil into a skillet and heat it over medium heat.
5. Coat the pork chops in the breadcrumb mixture carefully.
6. Fry the pork chops in the preheated olive oil for 10 minutes on both sides.
7. Chill the cooked pork chops.

Serving Suggestion: Serve with lemon wedges.
Variation Tip: Add paprika for more flavor.
Nutritional Information per Serving:
Calories 574 | Fat 34.1g | Sodium 1608mg | Carbs 14.1g | Fiber 1g | Sugar 1.1g | Protein 51.3g

Herbed Lamb Cutlets

Prep Time: 10 Minutes
Cook Time: 45 Minutes
Serves: 6

Ingredients:
- 2 red bell peppers, seeded and cut into chunks
- 1 large sweet potato, peeled and cut into chunks
- 2 zucchinis, sliced into chunks
- 1 red onion, cut into wedges
- 1 tablespoon olive oil
- 8 lean lamb cutlets, fat trimmed
- 1 tablespoon fresh thyme, chopped
- 2 tablespoons mint leaves, chopped
- Ground black pepper, to taste

Preparation:
1. Preheat the oven to 392°F.
2. Take a large-sized baking dish and add the bell peppers, zucchinis, sweet potatoes, and onion. Drizzle the oil all over them and season with some ground pepper.
3. Roast in the preheated oven for about 25 minutes.
4. Mix the herbs with a few more twists of ground black pepper and pat the mixture all over the cutlets.
5. Take the veggies out of the oven and put them to one side of the dish using a spatula.
6. Place the lamb cutlets on the other side of the dish and roast for 10 minutes.
7. Turn the cutlets over and cook for another 10 minutes until the veggies are ready (lightly charred and tender).
8. Mix everything on the tray and enjoy!

Serving Suggestion: Serve with some roasted Brussels sprouts.
Variation Tip: Roast for a few more minutes until the desired doneness.
Nutritional Information per Serving:
Calories 429 | Fat 29g | Sodium 320mg | Carbs 23g | Fiber1.3g | Sugar 2.1g | Protein 19g

Chicken and Poultry Recipes

Healthy Chicken Salad

Prep Time: 10 minutes
Cook Time: 5 minutes
Serves: 4
Ingredients:
8 ounces chicken, cooked and diced
2 ounces walnuts, chopped
2 tablespoons green onion, chopped
For Dressing:
1 tablespoon lemon juice
2 tablespoons fresh cilantro, chopped
⅛ teaspoon Cayenne
½ cup mayonnaise
1 teaspoon curry powder
¼ teaspoon pepper
¼ teaspoon salt
Directions:
1. In a small bowl, mix together all dressing ingredients and set aside.
2. Add chicken, walnuts, and green onion into the bowl and mix well.
3. Pour dressing over salad and toss well.
Serving Suggestion: Mix well and serve.
Variation Tip: You can also add chopped pecans instead of walnuts.
Nutritional Information per Serving:
Calories 292 | Fat 20g | Sodium 394mg | Carbs 9.1g | Fiber 1.3g | Sugar 2.2g | Protein 20.3g

Oregano Grilled Chicken

Prep Time: 10 minutes
Cook Time: 20 minutes
Serves: 4
Ingredients:
- ½ cup lemon juice

- ½ cup extra-virgin olive oil
- 3 tablespoons garlic, minced
- 2 teaspoons dried oregano
- 1 teaspoon red pepper flakes
- 1 teaspoon salt
- 2 pounds boneless, skinless chicken breasts
Preparation:
1. Combine the garlic, lemon juice, olive oil, oregano, red pepper flakes, and salt in a medium bowl.
2. Divide a chicken breast horizontally to get two thin pieces. Repeat this process with the rest of the chicken breasts.
3. Put the chicken in the bowl with the marinade and let it sit for at least 10 minutes before cooking.
4. Place a skillet on high heat and add some oil.
5. Cook each side of the breasts for 10 minutes, turning regularly.
6. Serve warm.
Serving Suggestion: Serve with lemon wedges.
Variation Tip: Omit red pepper flakes for a milder taste.
Nutritional Information per Serving:
Calories 479 | Fat 32g | Sodium 943mg | Carbs 5g | Fiber 1g | Sugar 1g | Protein 47g

Chicken with Artichoke

Prep Time: 10 minutes
Cook Time: 8 hours
Serves: 6
Ingredients:
- 6 chicken thighs, skinless and boneless
- 1 teaspoon dried basil
- 1 teaspoon dried oregano
- 14 olives, pitted
- 10 ounces frozen artichoke hearts
- 14 ounces can tomatoes, diced
- ½ teaspoon garlic powder
- 3 tablespoons fresh lemon juice
- Pepper
- Salt
Directions:
1. Season chicken with pepper and salt and place into the slow cooker.
2. Pour remaining ingredients over the chicken.
3. Cover and cook on low for 8 hours.
Serving Suggestion: Allow to cool completely then serve.
Variation Tip: Add 1 small sliced onion.
Nutritional Information per Serving:
Calories 329 | Fat 12.1g | Sodium 429mg | Carbs 9.5g | Fiber 4.2g | Sugar 3g | Protein 44.6g

Greek Roasted Pepper Chicken

Prep Time: 10 minutes
Cook Time: 4 hours
Serves: 6
Ingredients:
2 pounds chicken thighs, skinless and boneless
½ cup chicken stock
¾ cup olives
1 teaspoon oregano
1 cup roasted red peppers, chopped
1 tablespoon garlic, minced
1 tablespoon capers
1 teaspoon rosemary
1 teaspoon dried thyme
1 tablespoon olive oil
½ cup onion, sliced
Pepper
Salt
Directions:
1. Heat oil in a pan over medium-high heat.
2. Add chicken and cook until browned.
3. Add garlic and onion and cook for 5 minutes.
4. Transfer the chicken mixture into the slow cooker along with the remaining ingredients.
5. Cover and cook on low for 4 hours.
Serving Suggestion: Allow to cool completely then serve.
Variation Tip: Add your choice of seasonings.
Nutritional Information per Serving:
Calories 344 | Fat 15.5g | Sodium 484mg | Carbs 4.8g | Fiber 1.5g | Sugar 1.9g | Protein 44.5g

Grill Lemon Chicken

Prep Time: 10 minutes
Cook Time: 12 minutes
Serves: 4
Ingredients:
2 pounds chicken breasts, halves
1 teaspoon paprika
4 garlic cloves, minced

1 ½ teaspoon dried oregano
6 tablespoons olive oil
6 tablespoons fresh lemon juice
6 tablespoons fresh parsley, minced
Pepper
Salt
Directions:
1. Season chicken with pepper and salt.
2. Add chicken and remaining ingredients into the zip-lock bag. Seal bag and place in refrigerator for 1 hour.
3. Preheat the grill.
4. Place marinated chicken on the grill and cook for 5-6 minutes on each side.
Serving Suggestion: Allow to cool completely and serve.
Variation Tip: Add 1 teaspoon of Italian seasonings.
Nutritional Information per Serving:
Calories 626 | Fat 38.2g | Sodium 242mg | Carbs 2.5g | Fiber 0.8g | Sugar 0.6g | Protein 66.3g

Grilled Harissa Chicken

Prep Time: 10 minutes
Cook Time: 12 minutes
Serves: 2
Ingredients:
- Juice of 1 lemon
- 1 red onion, sliced
- 1½ teaspoons ground coriander
- 1½ teaspoons smoked paprika
- 1 teaspoon cumin
- 2 teaspoons cayenne pepper
- 3 tablespoons olive oil
- Kosher salt, to taste
- 8 boneless chicken thighs
- 2 tablespoons harissa paste
Preparation:
1. In a large bowl, add the chicken, olive oil, salt, onion, garlic, coriander, cumin, cayenne, lemon juice, and harissa paste, then mix well until the chicken is fully coated.
2. Place the oven rack 4 inches from the heat source. Preheat the broiler. Place the chicken on a broiler pan.
3. Broil each side of the chicken for about 7 minutes. The thickest part of the cooked chicken's temperature should read as 165℉ on a thermometer.
Serving Suggestion: Serve with a salad of your choice.
Variation Tip: For a milder taste, omit the cayenne pepper.
Nutritional Information per Serving:
Calories 142.5| Fat 4.7g | Sodium 102mg | Carbs 1.7g | Fiber 2.5g | Sugar 5.6g | Protein 22.1g

Chicken with Yogurt-Mint Sauce

Prep Time: 25 minutes
Cook Time: 25minutes
Serves: 4

Ingredients:
- 1 cup low-fat plain Greek yogurt
- 1 onion, finely chopped
- 1 tablespoon fresh mint, chopped
- 1 teaspoon fresh dill, chopped
- 1 teaspoon garlic, minced
- 1 teaspoon ground cumin
- Pinch of red pepper flakes
- 4 (3-ounce) boneless, skinless chicken breasts

Preparation:
1. In a medium bowl, whisk together the yogurt, onion, mint, dill, garlic, cumin, and red pepper flakes until blended.
2. Transfer ½ cup of the yogurt to a small bowl. Set aside, covered, in the refrigerator.
3. Add the chicken to the remaining yogurt mixture, turning to coat.
4. Cover and place the chicken in the refrigerator to marinate for 3 hours.
5. Preheat the oven to 400°F.
6. Transfer the chicken breasts to a baking sheet and roast until the chicken is cooked through, 25 minutes.
7. Serve with the reserved yogurt-mint sauce.

Serving Suggestion: Garnish with rosemary sprigs.
Variation Tip: Substitute the chicken breast with turkey breast.
Nutritional Information per Serving:
Calories 136 | Fat 7.6g | Sodium 82mg | Carbs 5.7g | Fiber 1g | Sugar 3g | Protein 26g

Feta Turkey Meatballs

Prep Time: 10 minutes
Cook Time: 20 minutes
Serves: 6

Ingredients:
1 egg, lightly beaten
2 pounds ground turkey
4 ounces Feta cheese, crumbled
1 tablespoon fresh mint, chopped

¼ teaspoon cumin
½ teaspoon onion powder
½ cup almond flour
¼ cup fresh parsley, chopped
1 cup spinach, chopped
½ teaspoon oregano
½ teaspoon pepper
Salt

Directions:
1. Preheat the oven to 450° F.
2. Add ground turkey and remaining ingredients into the large bowl and mix until well combined.
3. Make small balls from the meat mixture and place onto the baking sheet.
4. Bake for 20 minutes.

Serving Suggestion: Allow to cool completely and serve.
Variation Tip: You can use crumbled Goat cheese instead of Feta cheese.
Nutritional Information per Serving:
Calories 373 | Fat 22.6g | Sodium 417mg | Carbs 2.2g | Fiber 0.6g | Sugar 1g | Protein 45.8g

Caprese Chicken

Prep Time: 10 Minutes
Cook Time: 20 Minutes
Serves: 4

Ingredients:
- 2 boneless chicken breasts, sliced
- Salt and black pepper, to taste
- 1 tablespoon olive oil
- 1 tablespoon extra-virgin olive oil
- 6 ounces pesto
- 8 tomatoes, chopped
- 6mozzarella cheese, grated
- Balsamic glaze, as needed
- Kosher salt, to taste
- Fresh basil, as required

Preparation:
1. Preheat the oven to 400°F.
2. Mix the salt, sliced chicken, and pepper in a bowl. Set aside for 10 minutes.
3. Melt the olive oil in a skillet over medium heat.
4. Cook the chicken pieces in the melted olive oil for 5 minutes on each side. Remove from the heat.
5. Spread the pesto over the chicken and place the mozzarella cheese and tomatoes on top.
6. Bake in the preheated oven for 12 minutes.
7. Serve and enjoy.

Serving Suggestion: Garnish with balsamic glaze and basil.
Variation Tip: Chicken breasts can be substituted with chicken legs.
Nutritional Information per Serving:
Calories 232 | Fat 15g | Sodium 254mg | Carbs 5g | Fiber 1g | Sugar 5.7g | Protein 18g

Buttered Creamy Chicken

Prep Time: 10 minutes
Cook Time: 20 minutes
Serves: 4

Ingredients:
- ½ cup heavy whipping cream
- 1 tablespoon salt
- ½ cup bone broth
- Salt and black pepper, to taste
- 4 tablespoons cashew butter
- 4 chicken breast halves

Preparation:
1. Place a pan with one tablespoon of the cashew butter on medium heat.
2. Once the cashew butter is warm and melted, place the chicken in and cook for 7 minutes on each side.
3. Once the chicken is cooked through and golden, place it on a plate.
4. Add the bone broth, heavy whipping cream, salt, and pepper into the warm pan, and let the sauce simmer.
5. In about 5 minutes, the sauce should thicken up.
6. Add the rest of the cashew butter and the chicken back into the pan.
7. Spoon the sauce over the chicken and cover it completely.
8. Serve and enjoy!

Serving Suggestion: Top with chopped fresh parsley.
Variation Tip: Switch up cashew butter with any other nut butter.
Nutritional Information per Serving:
Calories 350 | Fat 25g | Sodium 394mg | Carbs 17g | Fiber 10g | Sugar 2g | Protein 25g

Turkey Meatballs

Prep Time: 10 minutes
Cook Time: 25 minutes
Serves: 2

Ingredients:
- 1 yellow onion, diced

- 14 ounces artichoke hearts, diced
- 1-pound ground turkey
- 1 teaspoon dried parsley
- 1 teaspoon olive oil
- 4 tablespoons basil, chopped
- Salt and pepper, to taste

Preparation:
1. Preheat the oven to 350℉. Grease a baking sheet.
2. Place the artichokes in a pan, add the oil, and sauté with the diced onions over medium heat for 5 minutes or until the onions are soft.
3. Meanwhile, mix the parsley, basil, and ground turkey with your hands in a big bowl. Season to taste.
4. Once the onion mixture has cooled, add it into the bowl and mix thoroughly.
5. With an ice cream scooper, scoop the ground turkey mixture and form balls.
6. Place the balls on the prepared baking sheet, pop in the oven, and bake until cooked (around 17 minutes).
7. Serve and enjoy.

Serving Suggestion: Serve over hot rice.
Variation Tip: Substitute turkey with chicken.
Nutritional Information per Serving:
Calories 283 | Fat 12g | Sodium 232mg | Carbs 30g | Fiber 12g | Sugar 4.3g | Protein 12g

Chicken Cacciatore

Prep Time: 10 Minutes
Cook Time: 39 Minutes
Serves: 8

Ingredients:
- 2 tablespoons extra-virgin olive oil
- 1 medium onion, chopped
- 3 tablespoons garlic, chopped
- 1 whole sized chicken, cut into 8 pieces
- 1 medium carrot, cubed
- 1 medium potato, cubed
- 1 medium red bell pepper, thinly sliced
- 2 cups stewed tomatoes
- 1 cup tomato sauce
- ½ cup green peas
- 1 teaspoon dried thyme
- Salt and black pepper, as needed

Preparation:
1. Place a large saucepan over medium-high heat.
2. Add the oil and allow it to heat up.
3. Stir in the garlic and onion and cook for 2 minutes.
4. Add the chicken and cook for 7 minutes, stirring throughout.
5. Add the carrots, red bell pepper, potato, stewed tomatoes, tomato sauce, green peas, thyme, and mix well.

6. Reduce the heat to low and simmer for 30 minutes. Season with salt and pepper.
7. Transfer to a serving dish and enjoy!
Serving Suggestion: Serve on a bed of rice or mashed potatoes.
Variation Tip: Add chili for a spicier dish.
Nutritional Information per Serving:
Calories 281 | Fat 8g | Sodium 413mg | Carbs 14g | Fiber 3.3g | Sugar 9.6g | Protein 39g

Turkey Casserole

Prep Time: 10 minutes
Cook Time: 40 minutes
Serves: 8
Ingredients:
• 9 ounces mozzarella cheese, sliced
• 1 teaspoon salt
• 1 teaspoon chili flakes
• 1 cup tomato juice
• 1 teaspoon oregano
• 4 sweet potatoes, peeled and spiralized
• 1-pound turkey fillet, chopped
• 4 teaspoons olive oil
• 1 tablespoon garlic, minced
• 1 cup tomatoes, sliced
• 1 cup Italian parsley, chopped
• 2 tablespoons heavy cream
• 1 tablespoon almond butter
Preparation:
1. Preheat the oven to 365℉.
2. Sprinkle the turkey with salt, chili flakes, and oregano and mix well.
3. Melt the butter in a skillet and add the turkey. Cook the turkey for 6 minutes, stirring it frequently.
4. Take a big square casserole dish and coat it with olive oil. Add the cooked turkey.
5. Add a layer of sliced tomatoes on top.
6. Combine the heavy cream with the minced garlic and tomato juice and whisk the mixture.
7. Then put the spiralized sweet potato in the dish and flatten it.
8. Pour in the tomato juice mixture and sprinkle over the chopped parsley.
9. Bake in the oven for 20 minutes.
10. Put the sliced mozzarella over the cooked casserole and bake the dish for 10 minutes more.
11. Remove the casserole from the oven and let it cool briefly before serving.
Serving Suggestion: Top with chopped parsley.
Variation Tip: Substitute turkey fillet with chicken fillet.
Nutritional Information per Serving:
Calories 433 | Fat 11g | Sodium 710mg | Carbs 23g | Fiber 30.6g | Sugar 3.8g | Protein 17.15g

Braised Chicken with Artichokes

Prep Time: 20 minutes
Cook Time: 1 hour 15 minutes
Serves: 4
Ingredients:
• 4 chicken leg quarters
• 1 tablespoon olive oil
• 1 yellow onion, chopped
• 1 teaspoon salt
• ½ teaspoon red pepper flakes, crushed
• 10 canned artichoke hearts, drained and halved
• 8 fresh thyme sprigs
• 1 (16-ounce) can low-sodium butter beans, rinsed and drained
• 4 garlic cloves, chopped
• 1 tablespoon black pepper
• 4 cups low-sodium chicken broth
• 2 cups cherry peppers
• 4 tablespoons fresh lemon juice
Preparation:
1. Preheat the oven to 375°F.
2. In a heavy, oven-proof wok placed over high heat, heat the oil and sear the chicken for about 5 minutes per side.
3. Put the chicken onto a warm plate.
4. In the same wok, add the garlic, onion, salt, black pepper, and red pepper flakes and sauté for about 1 minute.
5. Stir in the broth and let it come to a boil.
6. Remove the wok from the heat and stir in the cooked chicken, cherry peppers, artichoke hearts, thyme sprigs, and lemon juice.
7. Cover the pan and transfer it to the oven.
8. Bake for about 1 hour and then add the beans. Stir to combine.
9. Divide chicken leg quarters into the serving bowls and top with the artichoke mixture.
10. Serve immediately.
Serving Suggestion: Serve alongside your favorite soup.
Variation Tip: You can also use chicken wings.
Nutritional Information per Serving:
Calories: 611 | Fat: 19.8g | Sat Fat: 4.8g | Carbohydrates: 74.4g | Fiber: 29.3g | Sugar: 9.1g | Protein: 45.8g

Italian Baked Chicken Breast

Prep Time: 10 Minutes
Cook Time: 18 Minutes
Serves: 6
Ingredients:
- 2 pounds boneless chicken breast
- Salt and pepper, to taste
- 1 teaspoon thyme
- 1 red onion, sliced
- 1 teaspoon dried oregano
- 1 teaspoon sweet paprika
- 1 tablespoon olive oil
- 2 garlic cloves, minced
- 1 tablespoon lemon juice
- Campari tomatoes, to taste
- Handful fresh parsley, chopped, for garnish

Preparation:
1. Preheat the oven to 425°F.
2. Place the chicken pieces in a Ziploc bag. Flatten the pieces using a meat mallet.
3. Place the chicken into a bowl and rub the pieces with black pepper and salt.
4. Add the lemon juice, garlic, oil, and spices and mix well to coat the chicken thoroughly.
5. Place the onions in an oiled baking tray followed by the chicken and tomatoes. Cover the tray with foil.
6. Bake in the preheated oven for 10 minutes.
7. After 10 minutes, uncover and bake again for 8 more minutes.

Serving Suggestion: Serve with a sprinkling of parsley over the baked chicken.
Variation Tip: Omit the olive oil and use butter.
Nutritional Information per Serving:
Calories 290 | Fat 11.5g | Sodium 138mg | Carbs 11g | Fiber 0.8g | Sugar 2.1g | Protein 35.9g

Turkey Cutlets

Prep Time: 10 minutes
Cook Time: 10 minutes
Serves: 7
Ingredients:
- 1 teaspoon chili flakes
- 2 pounds ground turkey
- 1 teaspoon salt
- 1 teaspoon ground black pepper
- 1 teaspoon fresh ginger
- ¼ cup spinach
- ¼ cup Italian parsley
- 1 tablespoon oregano
- 2 tablespoons garlic, minced
- 3 tablespoons olive oil
- 1 cup breadcrumbs

Preparation:
1. Wash the spinach and Italian parsley carefully, chop them roughly, and put them in a blender.
2. Add the oregano, minced garlic, chili flakes, salt, ground black pepper, and fresh ginger. Pulse the mixture for 3 minutes. Place the mixture in a large bowl.
3. Add the ground turkey and mix it up.
4. Make cutlets from the meat mixture and coat every cutlet in the breadcrumbs.
5. Pour the olive oil into a skillet and make it shimmer.
6. Put the cutlets into the prepared pan and cook them for 2 minutes on each side on medium heat.
7. When all the cutlets are cooked, dry them with the help of a paper towel.
8. Serve the cooked dish with garlic sauce.

Serving Suggestion: Serve with a salad.
Variation Tip: For a milder taste, omit the chili flakes.
Nutritional Information per Serving:
Calories 374 | Fat 21.2g | Sodium 588mg | Carbs 12.9g | Fiber 1.2g | Sugar 1.1g | Protein 37.9g

Italian Chicken Meatballs

Prep Time: 10 minutes
Cook Time: 32 minutes
Serves: 20 meatballs
Ingredients:
- 3 tomatoes, chopped
- Kosher salt and black pepper, to taste
- ½ cup fresh parsley, chopped
- 1 teaspoon dried oregano
- ½ teaspoon fresh thyme
- ¼ teaspoon sweet paprika
- 1 red onion, thinly chopped
- 1-pound ground chicken
- ½ teaspoon garlic cloves, minced

- 1 raw egg
- ¼ cup parmesan cheese, grated
- 2 tablespoons extra-virgin olive oil.

Preparation:
1. Preheat the oven to 375℉.
2. Coat a skillet with some of the extra-virgin olive oil and set it aside.
3. In a large bowl, mix the tomatoes with kosher salt and the onions.
4. Add half of your fresh thyme and sprinkle a little extra-virgin olive oil on it again.
5. Transfer this mixture to your skillet and use a spoon to spread it evenly.
6. Add the ground chicken to a mixing bowl, and add the egg, parmesan cheese, a little amount of extra-virgin olive oil, oregano, paprika, garlic, the remaining thyme, chopped parsley, and black pepper.
7. Mix the mixture well and form about 1½-inch chicken meatballs.
8. Arrange the meatballs in the prepared skillet.
9. Bake in the preheated oven for about 30 minutes.
10. Your meatballs should turn golden brown when ready.
11. Serve and enjoy.

Serving Suggestion: Serve with tomato sauce.
Variation Tip: Add a pinch of chili for spice.
Nutritional Information per Serving:
Calories 79 | Fat 4.6g | Sodium 74.7mg | Carbs 4.1g | Fiber 0.4g | Sugar 1.4g | Protein 7.8g

Garlic Chicken Thighs

Prep Time: 10 minutes plus 12 hours marinating time
Cook Time: 30 minutes
Serves: 4
Ingredients:
- 8 skinless chicken thighs
- ¼ cup olive oil
- 8 cloves garlic, smashed
- 1½ teaspoons dried thyme
- 2 bay leaves
- ½ cup wine (like sherry, marsala, or port)
- ½ cup chicken broth
- 2 teaspoons Spanish smoked paprika
- Salt and black pepper, to taste
- Fresh parsley, chopped, for garnish

Preparation:
1. Coat the chicken evenly with the smoked paprika, then refrigerate overnight.
2. Heat the oil in a large skillet over medium heat. Sear the chicken for five minutes until browned but not cooked through.

3. Add the smashed garlic and cook until fragrant and slightly browned.
4. Season with salt and pepper to taste.
5. Add the rest of the ingredients except for the parsley. Bring to a boil.
6. Let simmer until the sauce is reduced and the chicken is done (about 20 minutes).
7. Remove the bay leaves and serve.

Serving Suggestion: Garnish with the chopped parsley.
Variation Tip: You could also use breasts or legs if preferred.
Nutritional Information per Serving:
Calories 290 | Fat 8g | Sodium 368mg | Carbs 11g | Fiber 0.9g | Sugar 0.2g | Protein 28g

Mediterranean Chicken Stir Fry

Prep Time: 10 minutes
Cook Time: 25 minutes
Serves: 4
Ingredients:
- ½ cup pitted green olives, sliced
- 2 small tomatoes, chopped
- 1 onion, chopped
- 1 zucchini, chopped
- ¼ teaspoon red pepper flakes
- 3 cloves garlic, minced
- 1 cup brown rice
- 2 teaspoons olive oil
- 1 teaspoon dried oregano
- 1 teaspoon dried basil
- 3 cups water
- 1-pound boneless chicken breasts, cubed
- Salt and pepper, to taste

Preparation:
1. In a medium pot on the stove, bring the water to a boil. Add the rice and cook as per the package instructions. Remove from the heat.
2. Add the olive oil to a skillet.
3. Lightly fry the chicken until it's fully cooked. Remove from the heat.
4. Add the onion to the same skillet. Add the garlic, red pepper, basil, zucchini, and oregano.
5. Stir fry until the vegetables become softer, then season with salt and pepper.
6. Add the cooked chicken, cooked rice, and tomatoes, and olives.

Serving Suggestion: Garnish with chopped green onions.
Variation Tip: Substitute water with chicken broth.
Nutritional Information per Serving:
Calories 401 | Fat 13.3g | Sodium 248mg | Carbs 44.1g | Fiber 3.9g | Sugar 3.3g | Protein 38g

Chicken Liver Stew

Prep Time: 10 minutes
Cook Time: 15 minutes
Serves: 5
Ingredients:
- 1 cup brandy
- 1 pound chicken livers, rinsed
- 1 cup sherry
- Kosher salt, to taste
- ½ cup sour cream
- 3 tablespoons olive oil
- 1 tablespoon fennel, chopped
- 1 tablespoon chives, chopped
- 1 tablespoon parsley, chopped

Preparation:
1. Salt the livers, place them in a dish, cover the dish, and keep them in the refrigerator until the next day.
2. Remove the livers from the fridge and rinse the salt off.
3. Place the olive oil in a skillet.
4. Heat the oil and add the fennel and chives, stirring well. Cover the skillet and slowly cook for 7 minutes.
5. Increase the heat to high. Put in the livers, constantly stirring as you heat them for a few minutes.
6. Add the brandy quickly. Ignite it with a lit match. Cover the pan and add the sherry.
7. Add ¼ cup of the sour cream. Stir until the mixture is blended well.
8. Bring close to boiling, but don't boil.
9. Remove from the heat. Stir in the remaining sour cream.
10. Serve.

Serving Suggestion: Garnish with chopped parsley and serve with rice.
Variation Tip: Feel free to use other herbs.
Nutritional Information per Serving:
Calories 307 | Fat 19.1g | Sodium 113mg | Carbs 2g | Fiber 0.1g | Sugar 0.1g | Protein 23g

Bruschetta Chicken Breasts

Prep Time: 15 minutes
Cook Time: 40 minutes
Serves: 4
Ingredients:
- 4 (6-ounce) chicken breasts
- Olive oil cooking spray
- Salt and black pepper, to taste
- ¼ cup fresh basil leaves, chopped
- 1 teaspoon balsamic vinegar
- 5 small tomatoes, chopped
- 1 garlic clove, minced
- 1 teaspoon olive oil

Preparation:
1. Preheat the oven to 375°F and grease a baking dish with the olive oil cooking spray.
2. Season the chicken breasts with the salt and black pepper.
3. Arrange the chicken breasts in a single layer in the baking dish.
4. Cover the baking dish and bake for about 40 minutes.
5. In the meantime, in a bowl, add the tomatoes, garlic, basil, vinegar, oil, and salt.
6. Mix well and refrigerate until using.
7. Remove the chicken breasts from the oven and transfer them to serving plates.
8. Serve topped with the tomato mixture.

Serving Suggestion: Serve with your favorite pasta.
Variation Tip: You can use any variety of tomatoes that you like.
Nutritional Information per Serving:
Calories: 355 | Fat: 14g | Sat Fat: 3.7g | Carbohydrates: 4.7g | Fiber: 1.4g | Sugar: 3g | Protein: 50.3g

Peanut Butter Yogurt Bowl

Prep Time: 5 minutes
Serves: 4
Ingredients:
- 4 cups vanilla Greek yogurt
- 2 bananas, sliced
- ¼ cup creamy peanut butter
- ¼ cup flaxseed meal
- 1 teaspoon nutmeg

Preparation:
1. Divide the yogurt into 4 bowls and add the banana slices on top.
2. Microwave the peanut butter for 30 to 40 seconds and add it to the bananas.
3. Sprinkle the flaxseed meal over the top.
Serving Suggestion: Top with nutmeg before serving.
Variation Tip: Banana can be replaced with berries.
Nutritional Information per Serving:
Calories: 370 | Fat: 10.6g | Sat Fat: 2.2g | Carbohydrates: 47.7g | Fiber: 4.7g | Sugar: 35.8g | Protein: 22.7g

Strawberry Popsicles

Prep Time: 10 minutes (plus 4 hours for freezing)
Serves: 8
Ingredients:
- 2½ cups strawberries
- ½ cup almond milk

Preparation:
1. Wash the strawberries with cold water and remove their hulls.
2. Blend the strawberries and almond milk in a food processor until smooth.
3. Place the mixture into molds with sticks and let them freeze for 4 hours.
Serving Suggestion: Serve with low-fat yogurt.
Variation Tip: Almond milk can be replaced with any milk.
Nutritional Information per Serving:
Calories: 56 | Fat: 4.6g | Sat Fat: 4g | Carbohydrates: 3.9g | Fiber: 1.2g | Sugar: 2.5g | Protein: 0.7g

Peach Sorbet

Prep Time: 10 Minutes
Cook Time: 10 Minutes
Serves: 4
Ingredients:
- 2 pounds peaches, pitted and quartered
- 2 cups apple juice
- 1 cup stevia
- 2 tablespoons lemon zest, grated

Preparation:
1. Heat a pan over medium heat, add the apple juice and the rest of the ingredients, and simmer for 10 minutes.
2. Transfer to a blender and pulse.
3. Divide the mixture into cups and keep in the freezer for 2 hours before serving.
Serving Suggestion: Garnish with peach slices and mint leaves.
Variation Tip: Add a tablespoon of lemon juice for a tangier taste.
Nutritional Information per Serving:
Calories 182 | Fat 5.4g | Sodium 50mg | Carbs 12g | Fiber 3.4g | Sugar 29.2g | Protein 5.4g

Cinnamon Honey Apples

Prep Time: 10 minutes
Cook Time: 10 minutes
Serves: 6
Ingredients:
6 apples, peeled, cored & diced
1 teaspoon cinnamon
1 small orange juice
⅛ teaspoon nutmeg
⅓ cup honey
Directions:
1. Add apples and remaining ingredients into the saucepan and mix well and cook over medium heat.
2. Simmer for 10 minutes.
Serving Suggestion: Stir well and serve warm.
Variation Tip: Add ½ teaspoon of vanilla extract.
Nutritional Information per Serving:
Calories 181 | Fat 0.5g | Sodium 3mg | Carbs 48.1g | Fiber 5.7g | Sugar 39.9g | Protein 0.8g

Mint Strawberry Treat

Prep Time: 10 minutes
Cook Time: 50 minutes
Serves: 6
Ingredients:
* Cooking spray
* ¼ cup stevia
* 1½ cups almond flour
* 1 teaspoon baking powder
* 1 cup almond milk
* 1 egg, whisked
* 2 cups strawberries, sliced
* 1 tablespoon mint, chopped
* 1 teaspoon lime zest, grated
* ½ cup whipping cream
Preparation:
1. Preheat the oven to 350℉.
2. Whisk the egg and almond milk in a bowl.
3. Add the flour, baking powder, stevia, and grated zest. Mix well.
4. Add the whipping cream and stir for 10 more minutes.
5. Add the mint and strawberries, and lightly mix with a spoon.
6. Grease 6 ramekins with the cooking spray and evenly distribute the strawberry mixture between them. Bake for 30 minutes.
7. Let them cool, then serve.
Serving Suggestion: Top with sliced strawberries and mint leaves.
Variation Tip: Substitute stevia with a sweetener of your choice.
Nutritional Information per Serving:
Calories 274 | Fat 9.1g | Sodium 48mg | Carbs 41g | Fiber 0.9g | Sugar 3g | Protein 4.5g

Cinnamon Honey Baby Carrots

Prep Time: 10 minutes
Cook Time: 20 minutes
Serves: 4
Ingredients:
1 pound baby carrots
1 teaspoon cinnamon
1 tablespoon honey
1 tablespoon olive oil
Directions:
1. In a bowl, toss carrots with honey, cinnamon and oil.
2. Add carrots into the air fryer basket.
3. Cook at 375° F for 20 minutes. Turn halfway through.
Serving Suggestion: Allow to cool completely then serve.
Variation Tip: You can also add maple syrup instead of honey.
Nutritional Information per Serving:
Calories 87 | Fat 3.7g | Sodium 89mg | Carbs 14.1g | Fiber 3.6g | Sugar 9.7g | Protein 0.8g

Watermelon Berry Popsicles

Prep Time: 5 minutes
Cook Time: 5 minutes
Serves: 10
Ingredients:
3 ½ cups watermelon cubed
½ cup Greek yogurt
½ cup strawberries, sliced
1 ½ teaspoon lemon juice
½ cup raspberries
Directions:
1. Add watermelon and remaining ingredients into the blender and blend until smooth.
2. Pour blended mixture into the popsicle molds and place in refrigerator for 6 hours.
Serving Suggestion: Serve chilled and enjoy.
Variation Tip: You can also add lime juice instead of lemon juice.
Nutritional Information per Serving:
Calories 28 | Fat 0.3g | Sodium 4mg | Carbs 5.4g | Fiber 0.7g | Sugar 4g | Protein 1.4g

Pomegranate Granita

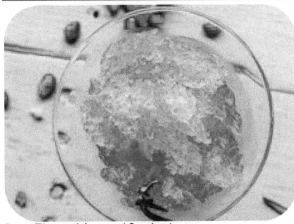

Prep Time: 4 hours 10 minutes
Cook Time: 0 minutes
Serves: 2
Ingredients:
• 4 cups pure pomegranate juice (no sugar added)
• ¼ cup honey
• ¼ teaspoon ground cinnamon
• Pinch of sea salt
Preparation:
1. Whisk the pomegranate juice, honey, cinnamon, and salt in a medium bowl until well blended.
2. Pour the pomegranate mixture into a 9-inch x 13-inch x 3-inch metal baking dish.

3. Freeze the mixture for at least 4 hours, scraping the surface with a fork every 30 minutes or so until the mixture looks like colored snow.
4. Store the granita in the freezer in a sealed container for up to 2 weeks, scraping with a fork when you want to serve it.
Serving Suggestion: Garnish with fresh rosemary.
Variation Tip: You can make granita with almost any type of juice or puréed fruit. Adjust the honey to suit the sweetness of whatever fruit you try in this recipe.
Nutritional Information per Serving:
Calories 205 | Fat 0g | Sodium 119mg | Carbs 56g | Fiber 0g | Sugar 54g | Protein 0g

Strawberry Crunch

Prep Time: 10 minutes
Cook Time: 55 minutes
Serves: 18
Ingredients:
• 1 cup white sugar
• 3 tablespoons all-purpose flour
• 3 cups fresh strawberries, sliced
• 3 cups rhubarb, cubed
For the crumble
• 1½ cups flour
• 1 cup packed brown sugar
• 1 cup cashew butter
• 1 cup oatmeal
Preparation:
1. Preheat the oven to 375°F
2. Mix the rhubarb, 3 tablespoons of flour, white sugar, and strawberries in a medium bowl. Put the mixture in a baking dish.
3. In another bowl, mix 1½ cups of flour, brown sugar, butter, and oats until a crumbly texture is obtained.
4. Evenly place the mixture over the fruit mixture in the baking dish.
5. Bake for 45 minutes or until crispy and light brown.
Serving Suggestion: Garnish with mint leaves.
Variation Tip: Substitute strawberries with blueberries or raspberries.
Nutritional Information per Serving:
Calories 253 | Fat 10.8g | Sodium 178mg | Carbs 38.1g | Fiber 12g | Sugar 8g | Protein 2.3g

Berry Yogurt

Prep Time: 5 minutes
Cook Time: 5 minutes
Serves: 4
Ingredients:
1 ½ cups blueberries
1 ½ cups blackberries
1 teaspoon lime juice
1 cup Greek yogurt
1 tablespoon honey
⅛ teaspoon salt
Directions:
1. Add berries, yogurt, honey, lime juice and salt into the blender and blend until smooth.
2. Cover and place in refrigerator for 2 hours.
Serving Suggestion: Serve chilled and enjoy.
Variation Tip: Add lemon juice instead of lime juice.
Nutritional Information per Serving:
Calories 111 | Fat 1.5g | Sodium 91mg | Carbs 20.3g | Fiber 4.2g | Sugar 14.6g | Protein 6.3g

Sweet Rice Pudding

Prep Time: 10 minutes
Cook Time: 50 minutes
Serves: 5
Ingredients:
• 2 cups water
• ¼ teaspoon salt
• 1 cup Arborio rice (sticky Italian rice), uncooked
• 1 stick cinnamon
• Rind of 1 lemon, in large pieces
• ¼ cup almond butter, divided
• 4¼ cups whole milk and about ¼ extra for egg yolks (if using)
• 3 egg yolks, beaten (optional)
• Vanilla extract (optional)
Preparation:
1. In a saucepan, combine the water and salt. Bring to a boil and then stir in the rice.

2. Reduce the heat to medium-low and simmer, stirring continuously, until the rice has absorbed almost all the water (about 20 minutes). Don't let it dry up completely so as not to burn it.
3. Add the cinnamon, lemon rind, half the butter, and the milk. Adjust the heat to medium-high. With continuous stirring, bring to a boil again and then reduce to a simmer.
4. Check for any rice that may have stuck to the bottom of the pan. Cook for 20 minutes.
5. Add the remaining butter and continue stirring while simmering for 10 more minutes. If using egg yolks (for a richer pudding), beat them well in a small bowl with the extra milk.
6. Pour this into the mixture gradually, mixing well after each addition. Cook a little longer to cook the yolks and thicken the mix further. Stir in vanilla (optional). Remove from the heat.
7. Discard the cinnamon stick and lemon rind. Pour into serving containers.
Serving Suggestion: Sprinkle cinnamon powder on top.
Variation Tip: May be served chilled or at room temperature.
Nutritional Information per Serving:
Calories 392 | Fat 10.5g | Sodium 215mg | Carbs 43.4g | Fiber 2.9g | Sugar 11.9g | Protein 11.5g

Minty Coconut Cream

Prep Time: 10 minutes
Cook Time: 0 minutes
Serves: 2
Ingredients:
• 1 banana, peeled
• 1½ cups coconut flesh, shredded
• 2 tablespoons mint, chopped
• 1½ cups coconut water
• 2 tablespoons stevia
• ½ avocado, pitted and chopped
Preparation:
1. In a blender, pulse the coconut with the banana.
2. Add the rest of the ingredients, and pulse well.
3. Divide into cups and serve cold.
Serving Suggestion: Garnish with mint leaves.
Variation Tip: Substitute stevia with a sweetener of your choice.
Nutritional Information per Serving:
Calories 193 | Fat 5.4g | Sodium 121mg | Carbs 7.6g | Fiber 3.4g | Sugar 15.4g | Protein 3g

Almond Bites

Prep Time: 10 minutes
Cook Time: 14 minutes
Serves: 5
Ingredients:
- 1 cup almond flour
- ¼ cup almond milk
- 1 egg, whisked
- 2 tablespoons almond butter
- 1 tablespoon coconut flakes
- ½ teaspoon baking powder
- ½ teaspoon apple cider vinegar
- ½ teaspoon vanilla extract

Preparation:
1. Mix the whisked egg, almond milk, apple cider vinegar, baking powder, vanilla extract, and butter.
2. Add the almond flour and coconut flakes, then knead the dough. If the dough is sticky, add more almond flour.
3. Make medium-sized balls from the dough and place them on the rack of an air fryer.
4. Press them gently with the palm of your hand. Lower the air fryer lid and cook the dessert for 12 minutes at 360°F.
5. Check if cooked; cook for 2 minutes more for a crunchier crust.
Serving Suggestion: Serve with a hot beverage of your choice.
Variation Tip: Switch up almond flour with coconut flour.
Nutritional Information per Serving:
Calories 118 | Fat 10.6g | Sodium 19mg | Carbs 3.6g | Fiber 1.6g | Sugar 1.1g | Protein 4.1g

Chia Seed Pudding

Prep Time: 12 hours 5 minutes

Cook Time: 0 minutes
Serves: 4
Ingredients:
- ½ cup chia seeds
- 1½ cups rice milk
- 1 teaspoon vanilla extract
- ¼ teaspoon cinnamon
- ¼ cup maple syrup

Preparation:
1. Add the above-listed ingredients in a bowl or a mason jar and mix well! Make sure the chia seeds don't stick to the container sides.
2. Cover the mixture and refrigerate overnight.
Serving Suggestion: Top with berries and mint leaves.
Variation Tip: You can also add fruit before serving.
Nutritional Information per Serving:
Calories 164 | Fat 6.2g | Sodium 37mg | Carbs 30.2g | Fiber 6.2g | Sugar 11.9g | Protein 3.1g

Cherry and Mint Sorbet

Prep Time: 3 hours 10 minutes
Cook Time: 0 minutes
Serves: 2
Ingredients:
- ½ cup maple syrup
- 2 cups cherries
- ¼ cup mint leaves
- 2 teaspoons lemon juice
- ¼ cup water
- ¼ cup coconut milk
- ⅛ teaspoon salt

Preparation:
1. Place the above-listed ingredients into a blender.
2. First blend on low and then at high speed to a thick and smooth consistency.
3. Serve immediately or store in your freezer for 2–3 hours to firm up.
Serving Suggestion: Garnish with mint.
Variation Tip: Switch up cherries with strawberries.
Nutritional Information per Serving:
Calories 426 | Fat 15g | Sodium 149mg | Carbs 79g | Fiber 1g | Sugar 73g | Protein 2g

4-Week Diet Plan

Week 1

Day 1:
Breakfast: Avocado Toast
Lunch: Cherry Tomatoes and Black Beans
Snack: Veggie Tortilla Wraps
Dinner: Herb-Crusted Halibut
Dessert: Mint Strawberry Treat

Day 2:
Breakfast: Vegetable Egg Cups
Lunch: Black-Eyed Peas Stew
Snack: Lamb-Filled Pita with Yogurt Sauce
Dinner: Bruschetta Chicken Breasts
Dessert: Minty Coconut Cream

Day 3:
Breakfast: Creamy Millet
Lunch: Cauliflower Rice
Snack: Butternut Squash Fries
Dinner: Chicken Cacciatore
Dessert: Chia Seed Pudding

Day 4:
Breakfast: Eggs Florentine
Lunch: Baked Black-Eyed Peas
Snack: Salmon and Celery Salad Wraps
Dinner: Italian Chicken Meatballs
Dessert: Pomegranate Granita

Day 5:
Breakfast: Cherry Oats Bowl
Lunch: White Beans with Tomato and Arugula
Snack: Peanut Butter Balls
Dinner: Halibut with Kale
Dessert: Cinnamon Honey Baby Carrots

Day 6:
Breakfast: Oat and Berry Parfait
Lunch: Sweet Red Lentils
Snack: Chickpea Spinach Patties
Dinner: Almond-Crusted Rack of Lamb
Dessert: Peach Sorbet

Day 7:
Breakfast: Avocado Milkshake
Lunch: Spelt-Stuffed Peppers
Snack: Carrot Cake Balls
Dinner: Turkey Meatballs
Dessert: Strawberry Crunch

Week 2

Day 1:
Breakfast: Avocado Milkshake
Lunch: Beets and Walnut Salad
Snack: Cauliflower Fritters
Dinner: Zesty Scallops
Dessert: Peanut Butter Yogurt Bowl

Day 2:
Breakfast: Vegetable Egg Cups
Lunch: Zucchini and Basil Soup
Snack: Grilled Veggie Sandwich
Dinner: Feta Turkey Meatballs
Dessert: Mint Strawberry Treat

Day 3:
Breakfast: Fruity Quinoa Bowl
Lunch: Lebanese Bean Salad
Snack: Bruschetta
Dinner: Grilled Lemon Salmon
Dessert: Cinnamon Honey Apples

Day 4:
Breakfast: Strawberry Smoothie Bowl
Lunch: Mediterranean Gnocchi
Snack: Avocado Caprese Wrap
Dinner: Grilled Harissa Chicken
Dessert: Mint Strawberry Treat

Day 5:
Breakfast: Almond Chia Porridge
Lunch: Black-Eyed Peas Stew
Snack: Zucchini Fritters
Dinner: Salmon with White Sauce
Dessert: Strawberry Crunch

Day 6:
Breakfast: Breakfast Chives Frittata
Lunch: Cannellini Beans and Farro Stew
Snack: Lamb-Filled Pita with Yogurt Sauce
Dinner: Braised Chicken with Artichokes
Dessert: Almond Bites

Day 7:
Breakfast: Cherry Oats Bowl
Lunch: Spicy Borlotti Beans
Snack: Crispy Chickpeas
Dinner: Herb-Crusted Halibut
Dessert: Mint Strawberry Treat

Week 3

Day 1:
Breakfast: Cheesy Potato Frittata
Lunch: Greek Avocado Salad
Snack: Easy Toasted Almonds
Dinner: Greek Roasted Pepper Chicken
Dessert: Sweet Rice Pudding

Day 2:
Breakfast: Quinoa Porridge
Lunch: Greek Chicken Gyro Salad
Snack: Butternut Squash Fries
Dinner: Grilled Lemon Salmon
Dessert: Pomegranate Granita

Day 3:
Breakfast: Creamy Millet
Lunch: Portuguese Salad
Snack: Salmon and Celery Salad Wraps
Dinner: Classic Calamari Stew
Dessert: Cinnamon Honey Baby Carrots

Day 4:
Breakfast: Veggies and Egg Scramble
Lunch: Beets and Walnut Salad
Snack: Chickpea Spinach Patties
Dinner: Garlic Chicken Thighs
Dessert: Almond Bites

Day 5:
Breakfast: Yogurt Bowl with Caramelized Figs
Lunch: Lebanese Bean Salad
Snack: Chicken Caprese Sandwich
Dinner: Easy Beef Roast
Dessert: Pomegranate Granita

Day 6:
Breakfast: Avocado Milkshake
Lunch: Beets and Walnut Salad
Snack: Carrot Cake Balls
Dinner: Clams Toscano
Dessert: Mint Strawberry Treat

Day 7:
Breakfast: Almond Chia Porridge
Lunch: Ratatouille
Snack: Avocado Caprese Wrap
Dinner: Octopus in Honey Sauce
Dessert: Peach Sorbet

Week 4

Day 1:
Breakfast: Tomato Omelet
Lunch: Pecan Salmon Salad
Snack: Zucchini Fritters
Dinner: Feta Turkey Meatballs
Dessert: Berry Yogurt

Day 2:
Breakfast: Yogurt Bowl with Caramelized Figs
Lunch: Cucumber and Tomato Salad
Snack: Peanut Butter Balls
Dinner: Salmon with White Sauce
Dessert: Peanut Butter Yogurt Bowl

Day 3:
Breakfast: Raspberry Oats
Lunch: Zucchini and Basil Soup
Snack: Butternut Squash Fries
Dinner: Almond-Crusted Tilapia
Dessert: Mint Strawberry Treat

Day 4:
Breakfast: Egg Breakfast Bowl
Lunch: Mediterranean Watermelon Salad
Snack: Zucchini Chips
Dinner: Greek Stuffed Squid
Dessert: Cherry and Mint Sorbet

Day 5:
Breakfast: Omelet Casserole
Lunch: Cauliflower and Farro Salad
Snack: Butternut Squash Fries
Dinner: Easy Shrimp Skewers
Dessert: Sweet Rice Pudding

Day 6:
Breakfast: Spinach and Egg Scramble
Lunch: Zucchini and Tomato Casserole
Snack: Easy Toasted Almonds
Dinner: Roasted Pork Tenderloin
Dessert: Cinnamon Honey Baby Carrots

Day 7:
Breakfast: Oat and Berry Parfait
Lunch: Greek Avocado Salad
Snack: Salmon and Celery Salad Wraps
Dinner: Zesty Scallops
Dessert: Almond Bites

Though there is no one-size-fits-all Mediterranean diet, it is generally high in healthful plant foods and low in animal foods, with a focus on fish and shellfish.

It has been linked to a variety of health advantages, including helping to regulate blood sugar levels, increasing heart health, and improving cognitive function, among others.

The best part is that you may customise the Mediterranean diet to suit your needs. If you don't care for salmon or sardines but enjoy whole wheat pasta and olive oil, start putting together great Mediterranean-inspired meals with things you enjoy.

Making long-term, sustainable dietary adjustments is a requirement of the Mediterranean diet.

In general, a diet rich in natural foods, such as abundance of veggies, whole grains, and nutritious fats, should be the goal.

Anyone who doesn't feel satisfied with their diet should consult a dietician. They can suggest more or different foods to help with satiety.

Do you want to improve your concentration? Begin with a cup of coffee and a lunch of 100 percent fruit juice, a whole-grain bagel with salmon, and 100 percent fruit juice. Experts recommend the following in addition to eating a well-balanced meal:

- Have a restful night's sleep.
- Keep yourself hydrated.
- Exercise can help you think more clearly.
- Relax and clear your mind by meditating.

Appendix Measurement Conversion Chart

VOLUME EQUIVALENTS(DRY)

US STANDARD	METRIC (APPROXIMATE)
1/8 teaspoon	0.5 mL
1/4 teaspoon	1 mL
1/2 teaspoon	2 mL
3/4 teaspoon	4 mL
1 teaspoon	5 mL
1 tablespoon	15 mL
1/4 cup	59 mL
1/2 cup	118 mL
3/4 cup	177 mL
1 cup	235 mL
2 cups	475 mL
3 cups	700 mL
4 cups	1 L

VOLUME EQUIVALENTS(LIQUID)

US STANDARD	US STANDARD (OUNCES)	METRIC (APPROXIMATE)
2 tablespoons	1 fl.oz.	30 mL
1/4 cup	2 fl.oz.	60 mL
1/2 cup	4 fl.oz.	120 mL
1 cup	8 fl.oz.	240 mL
1 1/2 cup	12 fl.oz.	355 mL
2 cups or 1 pint	16 fl.oz.	475 mL
4 cups or 1 quart	32 fl.oz.	1 L
1 gallon	128 fl.oz.	4 L

TEMPERATURES EQUIVALENTS

FAHRENHEIT(F)	CELSIUS(C) (APPROXIMATE)
225 °F	107 °C
250 °F	120 °C
275 °F	135 °C
300 °F	150 °C
325 °F	160 °C
350 °F	180 °C
375 °F	190 °C
400 °F	205 °C
425 °F	220 °C
450 °F	235 °C
475 °F	245 °C
500 °F	260 °C

WEIGHT EQUIVALENTS

US STANDARD	METRIC (APPROXIMATE)
1 ounce	28 g
2 ounces	57 g
5 ounces	142 g
10 ounces	284 g
15 ounces	425 g
16 ounces (1 pound)	455 g
1.5 pounds	680 g
2 pounds	907 g